A SACRAMENTAL PEOPLE

My head you have anointed with oil;
my cup is overflowing.
Psalm 22

Michael Drumm and Tom Gunning

A Sacramental People

Volume 1: Initiation

the columba press

First published in 1999 by
the columba press
55A Spruce Avenue, Stillorgan Industrial Park
Blackrock, Co Dublin

Cover by Bill Bolger
Origination by The Columba Press
Printed in Ireland by Colour Books Ltd, Dublin
ISBN 1 85607 263 0

Acknowledgements

The English translation of the Consecratory Prayer from the Chrism Mass from the *Rite of Confirmation, Rite of the Blessing of Oils, Rite of Consecrating the Chrism* © 1972, International Committee on English in the Liturgy, Inc. All Rights reserved. The illustrations are taken from *Clip-art for Celebrations and Service* by Gertrud Mueller Nelson, © 1990, The Order of St Benedict, The Liturgical Press, Collegeville, Minnesota. All rights reserved. Used by permission.

Contents

To Joan Gunning and Aileen Young

Foreword

The Catholic Church in Ireland is undergoing dramatic change. For many, this upheaval is associated with the irruption of various scandals in the 1990s. These scandals have shocked everybody and left many people reeling and confused. Alongside these scandals, however, another kind of change, less sensational but equally significant, has been taking place. It is a decline in the ability of the church to touch the spiritual lives of people. More specifically, it is a crisis concerning the capacity of the sacramental life of the church as we know it to nourish the spiritual hunger of Christians today.

Commentators note that spirituality is alive and well in Ireland. Some suggest a spiritual renaissance is taking place in the lives of people. The curious feature of this spiritual awakening is that it is taking place in spite of, or because of, recent scandals in the church. The link between spirituality and the sacraments is absent in this new wave of spirituality. A psychotherapist recently pointed out that the spiritual hunger so many people experience at present is no longer seen as something adequately addressed by the celebration of the sacraments or fulfilled by the Sunday celebration of the eucharist.

What is the source of this anomaly within contemporary Irish Catholicism? Is it the presence of so much secularism and materialism, or perhaps the constant intrusion of a profane media into our lives, or the ever-increasing fragmentation of contemporary culture, or the drive towards the privatisation of religion? No doubt these possibilities, often cited, are aspects of the breakdown of the link between spirituality and the celebration of the sacraments.

The underlying thesis of this book is that a significant part of the current crisis in Catholicism is the failure to appreciate the profound links that exist between ancient rites of passage and Christian initiation, between ritual and sacrament, between life and liturgy. The focus in this book is on the way we celebrate baptism, confirmation and eucharist in the life of the church and how this might be improved in the future. Pastoral problems are faced and turned around into catechetical opportunities. A second volume is planned to address the sacraments of healing, namely reconciliation and anointing, and the sacraments of vocation, namely marriage and orders.

In this first volume, the authors outline the historical, liturgical and theological development of the three sacraments of Christian initiation over the centuries. They note how the early church maintained a fundamental unity between baptism, confirmation and eucharist. Different models of Christian initiation are explored and pastoral preferences outlined. A valuable catechesis of the Sunday Liturgy is presented. The authors highlight how the current divorce between spirituality and the sacraments can be overcome. A striking feature of the book is the presence throughout of a practical catechesis on the meaning and unity of these three sacraments. Not only does the book theologise about the sacraments but it illustrates how that theology can be implemented in a pastoral manner. The book concludes with two appendices – one with 'A Ritual to Celebrate the Threshold of the New Millennium' and the other with a series of 'Texts for Use with Rituals'. This book will be a most valuable resource for overworked priests in parishes, for busy catechists in schools, and for bishops on their annual round of confirmation ceremonies.

The origin of this book is worth noting. In 1998 Michael Drumm wrote a book entitled *Passage to Pasch: Revisting the Catholic Sacraments*. In this carefully researched text, Drumm outlines an anthroplogy and sociology of ritual that goes back to pre-Christian times in Ireland. He shows how this ancient experience of ritual provides an important backdrop for understanding the Christian sacraments. He establishes links between primal rites of passage and Christian rituals of initiation. He makes fascinating connections between the festivals of Lughnasa and pilgrimages to Lough Derg with the sacramental life of the church. This original and creative work by Drumm begs the question: how can these rich theological insights be applied in a way that is pastorally relevant, catechetically helpful and spiritually enriching?

The answer to this question is given in *A Sacramental People, Volume 1: Initiation.* The co-author of this book, Tom Gunning, is a graduate of Mater Dei Institute who wrote his Masters thesis on 'Redeeming Ritual: Christian Initiation and Primitive Ritual Form' under the direction of Michael Drumm. In the light of this postgraduate work in Mater Dei Institute, Michael Drumm and Tom Gunning have put together this valuable book on a pastoral theology of the sacraments of Christian initiation

A Sacramental People represents a new kind of Christian reflection – an exercise in collaboration between a theologian and a catechist that is at once theologically informed, pastorally pertinent and catechetically instructive. Perhaps even more important is the way it shows how the gap between spirituality and the sacraments of initiation can be bridged, and in this way it addresses one of the most serious challenges facing Irish Catholicism today. *A Sacramental People,* volume one, is full of creative ideas for all who are concerned about the future of Catholicism in Ireland, especially those involved in lay ministry, religious education and the celebration of the sacraments. There is rich fare here for the whole Christian community in very accessible form.

Dermot A. Lane
Mater Dei Institute of Education

CHAPTER ONE

Renewing Sacramental Celebrations: Ten Principles

The principles outlined in this chapter form the basis for the analysis of sacramental celebrations in the rest of the book. The hope is that we might approach the seven sacraments of the church with a renewed sense of the power and beauty of the Catholic tradition. These varied insights can be gathered under ten different headings. In studying them, one must remember that it is the teaching of the Catholic Church that the seven sacraments are like a door opening onto the very life of God. The problem is that many people perceive the sacraments as a closed door rather than the inviting threshold they are intended to be. We can invest all the theological significance we want in our seven sacraments, but if they do not impact personally and socially on the lives of the participants then much of their power will vanish. All of the sacraments have the power to speak meaningfully. We need to channel this power in a very human way so that people might discover in religious ritual an evocation and expression of the life of the Spirit. Given the re-awakening of interest in spiritualities in our contemporary world, it is imperative that the church renews its sacramental life so that its rich tradition might speak anew. The following pointers might give a renewed focus to the sacraments.

1. Threefold division

It is now the norm for the Catholic Church to divide its seven sacraments into three categories. There are the three sacraments of initiation (baptism, confirmation and eucharist), the two sacraments of vocation (marriage and holy orders) and the two dealing with healing (reconciliation and the anointing of the sick). Through the sacraments of initiation one becomes a full member of the church, the sacraments of healing address issues of personal failure, human limitation and life's sorrows, whilst in the sacraments of vocation individuals take on specific ministries and roles within the Christian community. For the purposes of our analysis of the seven sacraments, we will follow this tripartite structure. This volume is devoted to Christian initiation. The sacraments of healing and vocation will be addressed in a second volume.

2. Initiation as the key rite of passage

At the beginning of this century Arnold van Gennep spoke of rites of passage for the first time. These were rites associated with important passages or transitions in the lives of human beings – like birth, puberty, betrothal and death – and significant aspects of the cosmic cycle – like midsummer, midwinter, a new moon, a new year, even a sunrise or a sunset. These varied passages demand a letting go of the old and an embrace of the new. The rituals that become associated with these passages are intended to facilitate the participants in this process of dying to one personal context or cosmic situation and rebirth to another. Amongst the most important rites of passage are those associated with the initiation of new members. Institutions set demands (in terms of age or commitment or particular achievements) which must be satisfied before the individual is initiated into the group through the celebration of some ritual or other. When these rites lose their meaning or when people simply go through the motions of what has become an empty ritual, then the implications for the particular group concerned – be it a family or a club or an academy or a church or a nation – are critical.

In the Catholic Church, new members are initiated through the celebration of the sacraments of baptism, confirmation and eucharist. Having received these three sacraments, an individual becomes a full member of the church. In some countries this process of initiation was underpinned by the general culture so that there was little difference between becoming a Catholic and a citizen of the nation. In other countries where Catholics formed a minority in the general population, initiation into the church was an important badge of identity in what was often perceived to be a hostile environment; minorities tend to have a very strong sense of identity built on the foundations of the rituals of initiation into their particular community. In most western countries today, both of these supports for the Catholic Church have largely disappeared. With the general secularisation of society and the dominance of Anglo-American television values, the socio-cultural foundations of religious initiation have crumbled. Such a situation poses both problems and opportunities. The problems are obvious in terms of falling numbers, growing catechetical illiteracy, lack of commitment and no real sense of belonging. But the opportunity for renewal, linked to a re-discovery of the power of Christian initiation, also suggests itself. Pope John Paul II has often spoken of the need to construct a spirituality centered on baptism and its significance in the Christian community. This is one of the main themes of this book: that the church must now turn its attention to its rites of initiation if it is to be a vibrant institution in the future.

3. Valid and fruitful

Traditionally a distinction is drawn between the validity and fruitfulness of sacramental celebrations. Sacraments might be valid but unfruitful (e.g. children are baptised for socio-cultural reasons but are not raised in the practice of the faith; youngsters are admitted to confirmation because they have reached a certain point in the education system even though they have no relationship with the local Christian community; two people get married in church purely to avoid family tensions). Whilst it would be sheer arrogance to judge that a sacrament bears no fruit in the life of a particular person, it is surely true that in many cases, like those listed above, the sacraments are of little significance in the lives of the participants. This is not to call the validity of such sacraments into question – the child was indeed baptised, the youngster was indeed confirmed, the couple did indeed get married – but it does raise the issue of how these rituals might make a greater impact in the lives of these people. Another way of looking at this issue is in terms of the role of grace and faith in sacramental celebrations. There are two key points: (a) valid sacraments bestow grace and (b) the sacraments demand and nourish faith. Balancing these two principles has always proved difficult. If one emphasises grace to the neglect of faith then the sacraments should be freely available to all comers, but if one puts greater stress on faith then one is quite likely to exclude people from certain sacraments due to lack of faith. One way of dealing with this problem is to build a certain level of faith formation into the actual celebration of the particular sacrament. In this way the ritual itself becomes a means of nourishing the very faith that it demands. It is the core argument of this book that the manner and context in which we actually perform the sacrament has a crucial bearing on its likely fruitfulness in the lives of the participants and the broader Christian community.

4. Faith

The sacraments demand and nourish faith. Without it they are quite meaningless. Of course it is difficult to measure the presence or absence of faith and so it is the traditional practice of the Catholic Church to admit to its sacramental rites all those who request such admission. The very act of physically coming to the sacrament is taken as evidence of the minimum faith required. Whilst this is a perfectly coherent argument, it may appear less plausible in an era of growing secularisation. The cultural roots of religious faith are being gradually severed, leading to growing illiteracy concerning the sacred texts and symbols of the Christian tradition. Given this new context, pastors should presume very little when it comes to the sacraments. On this basis some will refuse entry to those who do not commonly practise their faith through participation in the Sunday Mass; other pastors would be loathe to follow such a strict criterion. Another possibility, and the one favoured in this book, is to build in very definite elements of faith formation into the actual celebration so that participation in the sacrament becomes a source of nourishment of the faith of all those present.

But the question of faith goes deeper. Christian sacraments should facilitate growth in discipleship. Otherwise they run the danger of being nothing more than part of a civil religion; rites which justify the *status quo* politically, socially and economically, where there is no bite and no critique of who we are and no challenge to become something else. Being a disciple of Jesus Christ will invariably mean being challenged to live in a counter culture. Believers need support to do this and rituals which go against the cultural grain will challenge and affirm them in their commitment. Such rites today will need to open people to the mystery of life, stirring the great powers of wonder and awe, creating small dynamic communities where people feel wanted and cared for. If we fail to address this issue then some of our folk will turn to other rituals and could do so rapidly and, amongst the young, in large numbers. The explosion of interest in new age type symbols and rituals raises serious questions for the church. Clearly Christian communities need to renew their sacraments so that our ancient rituals can nourish the lives of people today. From the wealth of our own tradition we must draw out things both new and old in order to nurture Christian faith for our times.

There is no more representative symbol of life in the western world today than the television set. This wonderful piece of technology gives the viewer access to worlds that were once dim and distant. But it does far more. It has changed our imaginative and symbolic environment. Television has become our culture; the myths, categories and rituals which we use to interpret our world come, in large part, from the all-embracing electronic dictator in the corner of the room. If the sacraments are to survive in this electronic privatised culture they will have to become part of a counter-culture which challenges the dominant values and symbols of the television world and communicates a different understanding of the human person. Furthermore, we need to rediscover the communal roots of the sacraments so that they can subvert the insidious individualism so characteristic of our age.

5. The community

The communal dimension of sacramental celebrations must be retrieved. Whatever the merits of privatisation in business and commerce, it is a fatal flaw in religious sensibility. This is particularly true of the Catholic tradition with its love of symbol and ritual. The assembly gathering for its celebrations is the very lifeblood of the church. The fact that many of these gatherings in cities have become so anonymous, in that the participants remain strangers to one another, poses serious problems for the sacramental life of the church. In the contemporary western world, even critical rites of passage like birth, death and marriage are becoming ever more privatised and dominated by the values of the consumer market place. How might these issues be addressed?

St Paul speaks of the believing community as God's building, as the temple in which God dwells (1 Cor 3:9, 16). Several centuries later, Christians began to identify the word 'church' with the building in which the assembly of Christians gathered for their celebrations. This was deeply unfortunate as it tended to undermine the true meaning of church as the community of believers. If we are ever to retrieve this primordial meaning of the word 'church' then we will have to create a sense of belonging and shared responsibility. Surely the best context in which to begin to do this is in the existing gatherings of the community for its sacramental celebrations. Of course there will be need at times to gather the community, or some of its representatives, for other purposes but the key place where Christians encounter one another is during their sacramental gatherings. This is why these occasions should become the focus for renewal in the church. The clear fact is that Catholics still gather in significant numbers very regularly; the inability to tap into this reality in order to deepen people's sense of church is a stark failure. To change this situation will demand new attitudes, so that silence and passivity are no longer seen as the norm in liturgy but are replaced by active participation. Despite the substantial efforts made since the Second Vatican Council, the day is still some way off when in most church buildings people would feel at ease talking to the person sitting beside them if invited to do so, or when the seats are no longer affixed to the floor in such manner that movement is very limited. We need to foster a sense in which people are consciously present to one another in a way that doesn't happen on a train or in a supermarket or in a traffic jam or at a bar. The liturgical assembly must be retrieved from the clutches of an all-too-private form of piety, as if it were an occasion when I go to sort out my affairs with my God in much the same way as I deal individually with my lawyer or my doctor or my hairdresser or my garage mechanic. The church gathering must be different in creating a sense of belonging and shared responsibility. The church does not exist primarily for the spiritual comfort of individuals but rather to build a community that witnesses to the values that Jesus preached.

The Second Vatican Council intended to do just this, as is obvious from the new emphases that it inculcated. We have begun to use a new language which gives more attention to communal participation. One might contrast pre-Vatican II and post-Vatican II as follows:

Pre Vatican II	*Post Vatican II*
clerical centred	community
sacraments received	sacraments celebrated
passivity of recipient	faith of participant
rubric and law	word and symbol
priest is another Christ	a community in the Spirit
other-worldly	this-worldly
church centred	Christ centred
seven sacraments	sacramentality of all life

But although we have unquestionably changed the language that we use, it is legitimate to ask whether very much else has happened. In fact it could well be that, in many parishes and other ecclesial contexts, matters have ended up worse than they were in that the new language is used but the old reality persists. As ever in human life, when language and reality do not correspond tensions inevitably emerge. These begin with low levels of frustration, rising to significant experiences of alienation and finally to expressions of complete hostility. It would be a great tragedy if the spirit of the Council fails to move beyond language so as to create new realities. In order to do so, the law and theology which underpins many aspects of ministry will have to be developed towards new horizons of partnership and shared responsibility. It is obvious to any observer that there are currently real tensions present within the church. Our sacramental celebrations should not exacerbate these, so care should be taken with language and demeanour in order to foster a sense of welcome and warmth for all members of the community. Even when people disagree sincerely on some moral or doctrinal issues, they can still participate in the sacramental rituals together. In fact it is crucial that they do so, for otherwise they might lose sight of what it means to be the body of Christ. To be a member of Christ's body does not mean that a person should only gather with those of like mind, but rather it places a demand on all believers to build a community of faith which bears witness to the kingdom of God.

6 The word

The word must precede the sacrament. Before people celebrate a ritual they need to be immersed in the story which underpins it. This is why we have a liturgy of the word in every sacramental celebration before the introduction of key symbols like bread and wine, water and oil, giving consent and laying on of hands. The intention is not that the word explains the symbols but that it sets a context in which the symbols might speak anew to this particular assembly. Symbols carry enormous power which needs to be released but the great problem is that whole cultures and churches can forget the significance of a particular symbol. Then we face the terrible temptation, especially for preachers, to explain the symbol. Such an undertaking is doomed to failure as symbols are not explanations but carriers of meaning and of story. Bread is not an explanation of anything; it is a reality in and of itself which can mean very different things to different people. It might symbolise hunger or plenty, sharing or selfishness, hope or despair. To retrieve the Christian meaning of a symbol we have no choice but to retell the stories at the heart of our tradition. Without these stories we are not a people, and without a community rituals are only empty repetitions. The key function of the liturgy of the word is to retell the story so that the symbol might indeed speak afresh in a particular context.

There are, of course, different stories to be told. But the great Christian story is that of the paschal mystery. The word 'pasch' has a rich history. It comes down to us in particular from the Jewish feast of Passover, though it seems to pre-date even that ritual. In Palestine of old, nomadic peoples celebrated the spring lambing season with the sacrifice of a yearling lamb in honour of the gods of fertility. In the story of the Jewish ex-odus from Egypt, the sacrifice of the lamb became salvific. Families were instructed to slaughter a lamb and to sprinkle its blood on the lintels of their doors. Then the first-born males would be saved from the destroying angel who would pass over their houses. As a result of this plague, the Pharaoh released the Jews from slavery and they passed over the Red Sea from slavery to freedom. Thus it was that the people were saved by the blood of the innocent lamb known as the passover or paschal lamb because the angel passed over the houses and the people passed over the sea. This became the great founding story of the Jewish people and has been cele-brated ever since in the annual feast of Passover.

For the early Jewish Christians, Passover became central to their self-understanding. Coming to terms with their belief in the death and resurrection of Jesus, they turned to the Hebrew scriptures to see if they could find some tradition that would help to interpret what had happened. In the story of the paschal lamb they found just such a tradition. As the blood of the paschal lamb of old was shed, so Christians began to speak of Jesus as the new paschal lamb through the shedding of whose blood the people are saved. Thus it was that the lamb became one of the first symbols of the newly emerging church. As the Jews passed over the Red Sea, so Christians would pass through the waters of baptism from slavery to freedom, from sin to forgiveness, from death to life. And Christians had a new passover meal in their eucharist. So we speak of Jesus during the Mass as 'the lamb of God who takes away the sin of the world'. This, the greatest of all Christian stories, needs to be retold. It is deeply unfortunate that in the English language we use the word 'Easter' instead of 'pasch'; as a result people have very little sense of the meaning of this key term. The only way forward is to tell the story in such a way that people will grow in appreciation of its significance. The best context in which to do this is during sacramental celebrations.

There are other aspects of God's word to which we should also give attention. The seven sacraments celebrate God as creator, the Son as redeemer, and God's Spirit as indwelling in human life. This is an awe-inspiring tradition of worship of the one true God before whom we bow rather than reason. But maybe we reason too much. Our church rituals are too cerebral and verbal. The task of evangelisation, of proclaiming the word of God, does not imply endless words; as we participate in these ancient rituals we must be creative. Archaism and creativity go hand in hand. We must tap the ancient wellsprings of word and symbol, music and dance, art and movement, if people are to hear the word anew. In today's television world, we must face serious questions concerning how our people will hear this word which is ever ancient and ever new. The seven sacraments will remain the key means of evoking and celebrating the sacred. But Catholics have always known that we also need more if we are truly to hear the word of God. As we seek to encounter the sacred anew we'll probably find that novenas in honour of the Sacred Heart, Padre Pio, the miraculous medal, etc, are less effective today than rites which celebrate the cycle of the seasons, the land, the harvest, personal development, the discovery of the indwelling God, the endless horizons of the inner life, the

social and political demands of the gospel. The more creative-
ly we celebrate these realities, the more likely it is that people
will indeed hear the word of God.

7. Sacred time

The time at which a sacrament is celebrated is all important.
The reason for this is that it gives meaning to the story which
underpins the sacrament. When this meaning is lost then the
various aspects of the story have to be explained over and over
again. Thus the early Christians gathered for many of their
rituals in the evening darkness, as a vigil in anticipation of the
Lord's return, and at these celebrations candles became important symbols. Easter evolved as a time for initiating new
members through the waters of baptism. Today we commonly light candles in daylight and must then proceed to justify
this rather meaningless gesture, and baptism has completely
lost its roots in Easter time which leads to all sorts of mean-
dering efforts to explain what the rite is about. Our pagan
forebears demonstrated much more wit. The crucial times in
the solar and lunar calendars became times for celebration.
But it would have been meaningless to try to transfer the celebration of mid-winter (around 21 December) to, say, mid-
October. How could one possibly replicate the reality of the
disappearing sun? Even more to the point, why would one
want to attempt such nonsense? As the Jews evolved from fertility rituals to worship of the one God, the sacred time of the
sabbath became all important: every seventh day was sancti-
fied by turning from daily work to the worship of the one true
God. Our Christian forebears were similarly in tune with the
rhythms of life; the church calendar developed as a cyclic way
of encountering the mystery of Christ's life, but Sunday was
Sunday, Advent was Advent, Christmas was Christmas, Lent
was Lent, Easter was Easter; it would be stupid to suggest that
one could interchange these festivals. But sadly something

very different happened to the sacraments. They have evolved in such a way that they can be celebrated any time. This causes huge catechetical problems as the meaning of the symbols has to be explained, whereas if the sacraments were enacted at relevant times then their meaning would be much clearer. That is why throughout this book significant emphasis will be laid on the time at which a particular sacrament is celebrated.

Sacred time is being squeezed out of existence by the power of big business. The outstanding example of this is the gradual undermining of the traditional Sunday in some western countries. Another case in point is the oft expressed desire of the business and education establishments to fix the date of Easter on a particular Sunday. The consumer mindset must organise everything in terms of efficiency, whereas the beauty of ancient rituals is that they have nothing to do with productivity. This is a typical clash of the modern need to organise time and the traditional celebration of important points in the cosmic cycle; since Easter is dated by the moon, the festival (and all the others that flow from it – Ash Wednesday, Feast of the Ascension, Pentecost and Corpus Christi) falls on a different day every year. To tie Easter to a particular Sunday will break its link with the moon and render the last vestiges of the lunar calendar redundant in the western world. This would be a great loss because it would rupture important bonds with the past and break what is for many people their last connection with the natural rhythms of the universe. If we follow such a path, time will simply become a commodity. To save it from this fate we need sacred times in all of our lives. Protecting these times might be more important than we think; they may in the end be all that save us from total enslavement to the computer and the television.

8. Sacred space

If time is important, so too is space. All of the cosmos is holy
ground, but we need to erect sacred spaces to awaken us to this
reality. Some of the greatest buildings in the world – the
Pantheon and St Peter's Basilica in Rome, Hagia Sophia in
Istanbul, the Dome of the Rock in Jerusalem – open up a space
in which we can encounter the transcendent since they are big
enough to include all, high enough to awaken a sense of other-
ness, and yet small enough to remind us that we need the community to accompany us on our pilgrim way. But whatever of
these architectural gems, we all have need of holy places in our
own lives, sanctuaries to which we can withdraw in order to get
a different perspective on things. Without such spaces we are
likely to degenerate into little more than automatons. As ever,
we have much to learn from primitive societies. In the celebration of fertility rites certain places were all important because
they heightened the consciousness of participants of the fertility
of the earth. The classic centres for such rituals were the mountain top and the well and, as a result, these became sacred
places. In the case of mountains or hills, the height was not important but rather the breadth of the view over the surrounding
area, as this awakened a sense of the beauty and fertility of the
earth. Wells are sacred in all pre-modern societies, as water is
the most important gift that the earth provides. Similarly, pilgrimage centres, uninhabited islands, the seafront and monas-
teries became retreats from quotidian preoccupations. These
places are thresholds from which we can view life in a different
way from the norm, where there is the possibility of encountering the immeasurable and transformative forces of the unconscious and the sacred. Ordinary life is routine, functional
and often tedious. But the one-dimensional preoccupations of
everyday life can be blown away by the awesomeness of the
mountain-top; its predictability washed away by the ever

changing power of the ocean; its noise quietened in the silence of the cloister or the church; its emptiness filled by the solitude of the island; its loneliness embraced in the encounter with fellow pilgrims; its finiteness questioned by the endless gurgling of new waters from the well. All of us need such experiences to nourish the life of the spirit.

These varied examples demonstrate the importance of sacred spaces in human life. In attempting to renew the sacramental life of the church, this issue must be addressed. What are the sacred places in the lives of people today? The theatre? The sport's arena? The psychotherapist's chair? Can the local church building truly be a sacred space in the lives of the faithful? What could be done to enhance it in this regard? Should sacraments be celebrated in other places apart from churches?

9. Encounter

Christians believe that in human life we encounter the divine. There are different ways of doing so (see diagram overleaf). There is what we might call the direct path to the divine through meditation, personal prayer, contemplation, or, in more contemporary language, consciousness raising. The greatest mystics in history have travelled this path. We all need such reflection in our lives but this is a difficult journey and one that people often abandon through frustration, emptiness or despair. Those who have written about it from a Christian perspective do not paint a rosy picture but speak of the hard road to the high mountain or the distant shore or the inaccessible island where, bereft of all egoism, we encounter the divine in solitude and emptiness. Such experiences are simultaneously barren and ecstatic. The way of mystical union is ignored by most of us for it is too demanding and the cost of abandoning our egotistical desires and ambitions is simply too great.

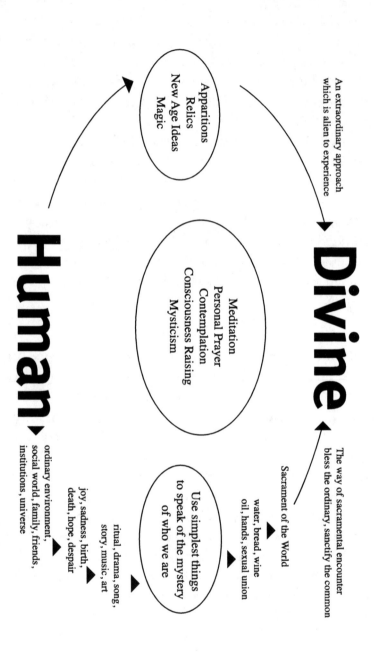

An extraordinary approach which is alien to experience

Apparitions
Relics
New Age Ideas
Magic

Divine

Meditation
Personal Prayer
Contemplation
Consciousness Raising
Mysticism

The way of sacramental encounter
bless the ordinary, sanctify the common

Sacrament of the World

water, bread, wine
oil, hands, sexual union

Use simplest things
to speak of the mystery
of who we are

ritual, drama, song,
story, music, art

joy, sadness, birth,
death, hope, despair

ordinary environment,
social world, family, friends,
institutions, universe

Human

There is a second way of encountering the divine. This is an extraordinary approach which is alien to experience. Given the difficulties and heartbreak of our lives, we turn our backs on the ordinary in the hope of encountering the divine. We place our trust in apparitions, relics, magic and increasingly in new age type mantras, crystals and tarot cards. Life can simply be too hard or too boring and so people reach out to strange forces in the hope that magic will intervene to change their lives. Whether one believes in these strange forces will vary from one person to another, but it is clear that they are not the best Christian understanding of the human encounter with the divine. That is better understood in terms of personal prayer and sacramental encounter.

The sacraments turn our attention towards human experience in a new way. To truly encounter the divine we must treasure our own humanity. Just look at what happens (follow the diagram). The human world that each of us inhabits is contextualised by family, friends, institutions of all forms (political, religious, educational), employment (or lack of) and the very universe itself. Within these various contexts we experience the most important realities in life – birth and death, joy and sadness, hope and despair, friendship and loneliness, love and hate. These intense experiences are celebrated and re-enacted in ritual and drama, song and story, music and art. Christian rituals use the simplest things to speak of the mystery of who we are. Through water, bread, wine, oil, hands and sexual union, we encounter the divine. This is what it means to speak of the sacrament of the world. Of course these very same realities can represent the exact opposite of what Christians intend, but water can give life, bread can nourish, wine can bring joy, oil can give a new fragrance, hands can affirm and bless, sexual union can be the fulness of committed love. But in the sacraments these realities are no longer just human but an actual encounter with the divine, as the waters of baptism give us a share in God's life and wash sin away, the oil of baptism and confirmation anoints us with God's Spirit, the bread and wine become the body and blood of Christ, the words of absolution bestow God's forgiveness, the oil of the sick opens the door to divine healing, the hand-laying and oil of ordination grant a special share in the priest-hood of Christ, and the giving of consent in marriage creates a bond that cannot be broken.

Notice that in sacramental encounter we bless the ordinary and sanctify the common. We are not asked to turn our backs on the world or on our human experience but rather to en-counter these realities in a new way. Nowhere is this better ex-pressed than in the preparation of the gifts at Mass where the priest says:

> Blessed are you, Lord, God of all creation. Through your goodness we have this bread to offer, which earth has given and human hands have made. It will become for us the bread of life.
> Blessed are you, Lord, God of all creation. Through your goodness we have this wine to offer, fruit of the vine and work of human hands. It will become our spiritual drink.

Christians believe that God has laid hold of humanity and has begun to transform us from within. Of course we can look at water, bread, wine, oil and see nothing of the miracle of human life, but our eyes can be opened and we can encounter in these simple things the divine depths of our lives.

10. Anticipating the kingdom of God

The sacraments are all about the future. Jesus preached the coming kingdom of God when the blind would see, the deaf would hear, the lame would walk and the dumb would speak. Our sacramental gatherings should be anticipations of this future where already the transformation of our material world into something divine has begun. Through the power of God's Holy Spirit the simplest of human realities are bearers of the divine. What the bread and wine become in the eucharist is a foretaste of the destiny of all reality – it will become Godly.

On our journey to the kingdom of God, we are very akin to the disciples on the road to Emmaus. At times we will be disappointed and frustrated; our hearts might even be downcast. We will need to hear the word; we will need to encounter others, including strangers; we will need to share meals together. Now and again we will see things differently, and whenever we do we will want to tell others, we will seek out Christian community. This is the unending story of Christian history. Jesus preached the kingdom of God. The rejection of him and his message led to his death on the cross. But a community formed around the belief that Jesus was raised from the dead, that death couldn't hold him. This community, the church, only exists to bear witness to the values of Jesus and to prepare the way for God's kingdom. From the beginning, believers gathered together for baptism and the breaking of bread. In the waters of baptism and the bread and wine of the eucharist they already encountered the divine destiny of the world. This community did not so much look backwards to Christ as forward to his return when God would be all in all. In the meantime they, and we their successors, gather to listen to the word, to nourish our faith, to build the bridges of community, to encounter the divine depths of our lives and to anticipate our future glory while still crying out: 'Come, Lord Jesus'.

CHAPTER TWO

Initiation

Initiation refers to that process whereby a community incorporates new members into itself. All tribes and cultures have developed elaborate rituals and rites of initiation so as to pass on the wisdom, knowledge and beliefs which are vital to the wellbeing and survival of the group. In all societies these rituals present the myths and symbols which define the identity of that community and set it apart from all others. Effective initiation guarantees a cohesiveness and security and bequeaths committed members to future generations. Rites of initiation, therefore, should be lavishly celebrated, because at a very human level they become those rites that ensure a future for the whole group. If initiation is non-existent or fails, then the community will die.

Initiation as Dying and Rebirth

In archaic societies it was a constant, within the dynamics of initiation, that they always involved the symbols of dying and new birth as channels towards a deepening of the spiritual life. A guiding principle in initiation must be that nothing new emerges in a person unless a real inner dying first takes place. Genuine initiation must be disconcerting and difficult. In trying to renew its sacraments of initiation, the church could learn much from the rituals of primitive societies. In this context the word 'primitive' should not be interpreted pejoratively. It should not be understood as infantile behaviour but rather as pre-modern. Primitive rituals are the lifeblood of the tribe or the village, but they lose their meaning in the modern city. Still we have much to learn from them about the nature of ritual initiation.

One of the most significant insights to be gained from anthropological studies of primitive rituals is that initiation effects real change. Ultimately, this is the same claim made about the sacraments of initiation. In many primitive cultures, rites of initiation into adulthood were extremely difficult, as the forging of a new identity was a demanding task. The dying to the existing, familiar identity which transformation demanded, was understandably not something people chose to do voluntarily, so the power of ritual came from its ability to guide and facilitate the individual, within a supporting group, through this self-deprecating action. This was not intended to be an entirely pleasant experience but, in ritual, the higher the psychological price paid the more effective the result. This explains both the unsettling and painful nature of many rites of initiation and the need for communal support. When the rite was complete, those who were initiated into adulthood had been transformed by the power of the ritual and they lived and experienced their new identities recognised by all, as men instead of boys, women instead of girls. Quite simply, in the primitive world new identities were created by their rites of initiation, just as Tertullian remarked about Christians that they 'are made, not born'.

With the demise of primitive rites modern Christians only experience initiation through the sacraments. But many commentators argue that these sacraments have lost their 'initiatory aura'. This is a serious claim and suggests that our sacraments do not fulfil the requirements for a person to fully experience the dynamics of initiation, change and growth. The experience of spiritual regeneration, which pre-modern people discovered in initiatory rituals, needs to be encountered in the sacraments because true transformation requires both the pain of loss and the spirit of creative renewal. When this happens change occurs and a new person emerges transformed and regenerated. Life takes on new meaning because in dying to the old self a person profoundly experiences the divine. This may sound radical and uncompromising, but living in accord with gospel values is difficult. It corresponds with many of the practices of the early church where it wasn't easy to become a Christian and accordingly initiation into the church was difficult. Only through a process of letting go and adopting a new identity did people become part of a radically different community. What of the situation today? Has initiation into the Christian community become too easy? Is there any experience of going through the ache of loss and being transformed? Before we can address the contemporary scene, which we will in chapters three and four, we need to delve into Christian history in order to see how the story of the formation of new members has evolved over the centuries.

The Beginnings of Christian Initiation

If we look at various cultures, we encounter many and varied rituals of initiation. However, water rituals are most common and one such ritual of initiation is immersion in water, or what Christians term baptism. In order to better understand the nature of water symbolism and why we use water in initiation, we can examine the text in Genesis concerning creation. In it we read: 'Now the earth was a formless void and God's Spirit hovered over the waters' (Gen 1:2). It is from these primal and chaotic waters that creation emerges. Water is central when it comes to rituals of initiation because as an archetype it is the location of creation, transformation and new life. It is God's spirit in the water that changes, transforms and creates anew.

The origins of Christian initiation are to be found in the wilderness and in water. A man called John dressed in animal

skins preached repentance and forgiveness of sin. Hundreds
came to this strange character to be baptised. The word *baptism* comes from the Greek verb *baptizein* which means 'to
dip' or 'to plunge'. To meet John the Baptist meant leaving
the towns and villages and familiarity of ordinary life to be
plunged into the formless and chaotic waters of the Jordan.
Mark tells us that 'as they were baptised in the river Jordan
they confessed their sins' (Mk 1:5). This descent provoked an
awareness of their own sinfulness. Something died within
them as they plunged down and they departed from the river-
bank purified and forgiven. This form of ritual was not for-
eign to the Jews, as they already employed a type of water immersion along with circumcision as a rite of purification for
Gentiles converting to Judaism. Yet the purpose of John's
baptism with water was to herald the radically different baptism which Jesus would bring. That would be a baptism of
the Holy Spirit.

All the evangelists testify to the baptism of Jesus by John
the Baptist. In John's gospel the evangelist states that John the
Baptist was told by the one who sent him that: 'The man on
whom you see the Spirit come down and rest is the one who is
going to baptise with the Holy Spirit' (Jn 1:33). There was an
understanding within the early Christian community that
Jesus was endowed with the Holy Spirit and that he was therefore the one who could bestow this gift on those who followed
him. This shows that there was a significant development in
their understanding of baptism. Remember the early converts
to Christianity only had a purificatory understanding of baptism and one that went no further than John's baptism. But in
the Acts of the Apostles we are told in striking imagery of what
happened on the 'fiftieth day' (Pentecost) after Easter. There
was a dramatic metamorphosis within the community of the
followers of Jesus and with it came a dramatic development in
their understanding of baptism and initiation.

Pentecost is regarded as the birth of the universal church and it was a Spirit-filled event. In ancient Judaism, Pentecost was celebrated fifty days after Passover and it was the spring festival of first fruits. On the fiftieth day after the death of Jesus, tongues of fire lit up the darkened room and the disciples received the first fruits of the Spirit. Later, in a loud voice, Peter addressed the assembled crowd and declared that Jesus received the Holy Spirit from his Father and, 'what you see here is an outpouring of that Spirit' (Acts 2:33). Based on what happened on that day of Pentecost, and on many other occasions described in the Acts of the Apostles, we can identify several features that are central to a contemporary understanding of baptism.

(a) Word and Faith

Of primary importance to the whole process of initiation is the proclamation of the word. Peter addressed the crowd about the outpouring of the Holy Spirit and then declared that Jesus who was crucified is both Lord and Christ. 'Hearing this, they were cut to the heart and said to Peter and the apostles "What must we do, brothers?" "You must repent," Peter answered, "and every one of you must be baptised in the name of Jesus Christ for the forgiveness of your sins, and you will receive the gift of the Holy Spirit"' (2:37-38). In Acts it is clear that there is an inherent continuity between the proclamation of the word and baptism. To put this another way, within the process of initiation there is a continuous event between proclamation of the good news and faith in it: 'He who believes and is baptised will be saved' (Mk 16:16). Initiation therefore must take place within the context of faith, otherwise the ritual becomes redundant. Faith and baptism are inseparable.

(b) Community

There was a real sense that the context for becoming a Christian was communal. In fact the community is primordial within Christianity because it was that initial Pentecostal community that first proclaimed the word. Initiation into the church is a deeply personal affair but it is not a private matter, and so it should only be celebrated in a living community. Baptism exists not primarily for the comfort and encouragement of individuals but to create and sustain the life of the Christian community.

(c) Freedom from Sin and the Gift of the Spirit

The water baptism of John the Baptist entailed purification and repentance for the forgiveness of sins and this continues within the Christian tradition. But in the Christian community baptism takes on an added meaning as promised by Christ: 'John baptised with water but you, not many days from now, will be baptised with the Holy Spirit' (Acts 1:5). This text demonstrates that, within the consciousness of the early Christian community, baptism was not only considered as purificatory for the forgiveness of sins but it was also associated with the gift of the Holy Spirit. It is unfortunate that, in the later history of Christian initiation, baptism came to be understood simply as a rite of purification from sin. Baptism does indeed involve the washing away of all sin but the waters are not just cleansing but also transformative as the Spirit is poured out.

(d) Dying and Rising with Christ

Baptism has four effects and thus far we have recognised three: entrance into the communal life of the church, salvation from sin, and a sharing in the life of the Spirit. In his Letter to the Romans, St Paul highlights the other dimension of baptism as an initiation into the life of Christ. He writes:

'When we were baptised in Christ Jesus we were baptised in his death; in other words, when we were baptised we went into the tomb with him and joined him in death, so that as Christ was raised from the dead by the Father's glory, we too might live a new life' (Rom 6:3-4). This means that we are immersed with Christ in the baptismal waters and we enter a dynamic of death and new life. When we rise with him out of the waters of baptism we are called to live a new life: to forgive as he forgave, to serve as he served, to love as he loved and to always die to self for the sake of others. To enter into the life of the Easter Jesus, is to enter a life of constant transformation and change as mapped in the paschal dynamic of death and resurrection. This means that when one is initiated it is into a discipleship of self-sacrifice; that one is immersed into the reality of Good Friday, Holy Saturday and Easter Sunday. Any human can forgive, serve or love, but those baptised into Christianity enter the life of him 'whose power, working in us, can do infinitely more than we can ask or imagine' (Eph 3:20). If Christian initiation is to signify anything, it should mean that those baptised will live their lives differently from before. There is little point in becoming a member of a new group if nothing changes afterwards. Baptism must be seen as a process of radical change in one's life. The old self should die in the baptismal waters and a new self emerge. John Chrysostom (329-407) wrote that in baptism: 'When we plunge our heads into the water as into a sepulcher, the old man is immersed, buried whole; when we come out of the water, the new man appears at the same time.' As described in the first chapter of Genesis, something new emerges from the waters. This truth is echoed in St Paul's prayer for the community at Ephesus: 'Out of his infinite glory, may he give you the power through his Spirit for your hidden self to grow strong' (Eph 3:16). After baptism something should be different, something should have changed.

In Acts it is evident that there is a definite continuity between the water ritual as entrance into the life of Christ and the gift of the Spirit. While the external form of the ritual seemed to vary, what is certain is that the giving of the Spirit was tied to the ritual of baptism and water. In one instance at Samaria, Philip baptised the converts but they did not receive the Spirit until Peter and John came from Jerusalem and laid hands on them (8:12-17). In Caesarea, however, the converts had already received the Spirit and it was on the evidence of this that Peter baptised them (10:44-48). It is clear then that baptism was as much about receiving the Spirit as immersion into the paschal waters of a new life in Christ.

To summarise then, initiation originates in the community as a response in faith to the proclaimed word about salvation in Jesus Christ. To be baptised is to enter this same Spirit-filled community, which lives its life in a paschal nature imitating the life of Christ. Baptism frees one from sin and is a ritual that can alter one's life dramatically.

Initiation in the third century

In the centuries that followed Pentecost baptism and the process of initiation evolved and developed. What is interesting to note is how the essential features as outlined above became incorporated into the emerging rites. We get a good idea of what initiation was like in the third century from the *Apostolic Tradition* written by Hipppolytus in approximately 215 for the Greek-speaking church in Rome. What is immediately striking in this text is that it took three years for an adult convert to become a Christian. There was a definite sense of separation from an old way of life as the candidates had to prepare to live according to the values of the gospel. Once their motives and lifestyle were examined, they were admitted to the lengthy process of official formation and instruction called the catechumenate.

Those who had become catechumens were like people standing on the threshold between two worlds – their pagan past and the Christian future that awaited them. After the three years of catechumenate they underwent an examination, not with regards to knowledge but to conduct. If they passed it they were admitted to 'proximate preparation' for their baptism which would occur at Easter. This stage lasted for forty days and during their instruction they were required to fast, pray and keep long vigils. From the fourth century onwards, this time, called Lent, became a period of asceticism for the whole Christian community and not just the candidate. The faithful too were encouraged to align their lives with that of the catechumens so that the whole community annually entered a state of renewal and regeneration. This is the origin of Lent.

The period of the catechumenate was a time of preparation before entry into the community. The one preparing for baptism was immersed in the scriptures, beliefs and traditions of the church and introduced to the members of the local community. Baptised adults accompanied the catechumens on the spiritual journey from unbelief to faith. At the end of this period they were brought before the community on Holy Saturday night for the rites of initiation. At this most solemn gathering, the catechumens, almost naked, were brought before a presbyter (priest) who anointed them with the oil of exorcism to strengthen their faith in the midst of evil and unbelief. With this oil dripping from their bodies they proceeded to the baptismal pool or font, where standing in the waters they professed their faith in the Triune God and were immersed three times. Emerging from these life-giving waters the newly baptised were anointed with chrism which gave them the fragrance of Christ himself. In an extraordinary prophetic act, the church poured the oil of chrism on their heads, anointing them with the very Spirit of Jesus Christ.

Drowned with water and covered in oil, the neophytes were brought before the bishop who laid hands on them while invoking the Holy Spirit to come upon them. Finally they participated for the first time in the most intimate mystery of the life of the Christian community as they prayed with the faithful, shared the kiss of peace and were welcomed to the table for the breaking of bread where they partook of the body and blood of Christ. In the third century, then, one sees a well developed ritual highlighting several key dimensions of Christian belief.

It is important to note that a different tradition developed in some parts of the East. In the Syrian and Armenian liturgies of initiation the process involved an anointing followed by immersion in water and finally eucharist. This pre-baptismal anointing was quite definitely Spirit-filled and Messianic insofar as the presbyter invoked the 'Messiah' (which means the 'anointed one') and the 'Spirit of Holiness' before the immersion. If we compare the Eastern and Western liturgies it is clear that there was no definite sequence of events, even though there were quite evidently two aspects to the liturgy – baptism by immersion and anointing.

By the third century there was one complete ritual of initiation that involved the whole community during the paschal or Easter vigil. The different symbols used evoked the various aspects of becoming a Christian. Water signified the remission of sins, salvation and entrance into Christ's paschal life, whilst the anointings symbolised the gift of the Spirit and a sharing in Christ's own priesthood as the 'anointed one'. Whilst there were various features to the ritual of initiation, it symbolised and actualised the single yet mysterious event of entering the life of God – Father, Son and Holy Spirit. The question as to at what precise moment one actually became a Christian or actually received the Spirit seemed irrelevant.

We mentioned earlier that the entire Christian community

entered into the experiences of the catechumens in the early church. Clearly baptism as a commitment to a particular way of life was understood as a lifelong process which must be constantly revisited and renewed. Baptism wasn't understood as a once off, almost magical ritual. Instead the words of commitment and the symbols of adherence to Christ served to remind the faithful of what exactly it meant to be a disciple, a follower of Christ.

The ritual of initiation evolved and changed from the simple immersion and laying on of hands in the Acts of the Apostles to the more elaborate rites spread out over three years by the third century. So too differing rites emerged in the East and West. It is a simple historical fact that from the beginning there were various interpretations and models of how the community should go about the process of initiating or making Christians. After the third century the process of initiation would undergo even more radical changes and many different models were set to appear. One must analyse these changes in order to understand the way we initiate new members today.

At present we baptise at infancy, give communion at about seven years of age and confirm at various ages in different parts of the world. Over the last fifteen hundred years there has been a radical change in the initiatory policy of the Catholic Church. It might indeed appear that the present method is the only one, that history has somehow stolen from us an older more unified process, one richer in meaning, time, symbolism and fellowship. Thus we speak of the dissolution of the rites of Christian initiation. In doing so we refer primarily to the break-up of the process of initiation into the separate sacraments of baptism, confirmation and first communion. The story of the unravelling of the ancient unified rite is both complex and detailed but certain factors were central to its undoing.

The Dissolution of Christian Initiation

In the apostolic church adult conversions and baptisms were the norm even though some infants were baptised. The process of initiating adults obviously necessitated a long period of catechumenate but in the fourth century two factors were to change this. Firstly, after Constantine's conversion there was a huge influx of converts into the church and the sheer volume overwhelmed the catechumenate to such an extent that it was radically abbreviated. Secondly, due to his tussles with Pelagius, Augustine developed a theology of original sin which determined that those who were not baptised, even infants, were eternally lost. Parents, therefore, wanted their infants baptised as soon as possible after birth. Baptism became an emergency rite solely for the salvation of the child's soul. This was a crucial development because the catechumenate all but disappeared in order to save time. Baptism, appreciated simply as a purificatory rite, was stripped of the other dimensions that we identified above – immersion in the paschal life of Christ, the gift of the Spirit and entrance into the community of the church. Coinciding with this development parents were unwilling to wait until Easter to baptise their infants and so Easter was dropped as the preferred symbolic time to baptise. This further undermined the paschal significance of the rite. However, even with these dramatic developments there still existed a unified ritual of initiation but in time this too was to change.

From an early stage, the centrality of the bishop in initiation was well established. The bishop sealed the baptised with the oil of chrism and the laying on of hands. As Christianity became more popular after Constantine, parish priests were forced to perform baptisms in the absence of the bishop. But in the western church the bishops insisted on maintaining their role in the anointing and laying of hands on those who were baptised. Yet, with exploding numbers, bishops couldn't attend all baptisms except perhaps in Rome where bishops were plentiful. Consequently infants were baptised locally but then later brought to the bishop for the laying on of hands where he literally 'confirmed' the earlier rite performed by the priest. At a later stage they were admitted to the table of the eucharist. Reflecting on this separation, later medieval theologians inferred that the Spirit is conferred during the episcopal rites. This meant that the process of initiation was separated by time and place into three distinct sacraments: baptism, confirmation and eucharist.

Later, the church declared that only those who had reached the age of reason, seven years of age, could receive confirmation from the bishop. Baptism and confirmation were thus regarded as separate sacraments with separate ministers. The Council of Trent said that it was preferable that only those who were twelve years of age should receive confirmation as it would arm them better against the assaults of the world. Thus the rite of initiation followed the same pattern as earlier times except that now it could take up to twelve years to complete. At the beginning of this century, Pope Pius x sanctioned a new practice. He was perturbed by the small number of those attending Mass who received communion and so he reduced the age of admittance to the sacrament to seven years. In time the numbers grew but the effect on initiation was to overturn the traditional order and confirmation was postponed until after first communion. By this century, then, the rite of initiation was not only fragmented but also celebrated in a different order. The legacy of these developments is the contemporary model of initiation which is ordinarily used in most countries today. Those who are baptised as infants are admitted to first communion at seven or eight years and are confirmed at some stage between nine and fourteen years.

From the 1930s onwards, scholarly debate began within

both Catholic and Protestant circles over the role to which baptism had been consigned. It was being viewed as that sacrament peculiar to infancy, whilst confirmation was over emphasised as the sacrament of mature commitment to the church. Fortunately, what characterises twentieth century theology is a return to the scriptural and patristic sources of the early church. This movement placed renewed emphasis on the death and resurrection of Christ as the core of Christian belief. Translated into the language of sacramental theology it means that to celebrate any sacrament is to celebrate the Christ event. The difficulty was that baptism was perceived as a private ceremony concerning personal salvation. Whilst we are saved from sin through the waters of baptism the importance of community needed to be restated as the proper context for initiation. So too conversion and faith were reappraised as being central to the process of initiation. In the next chapter we will examine different ways of becoming a member of the church which attempt to give due weight to these various dimensions of Christian initiation.

CHAPTER THREE

Ten Models of Christian Initiation

Christians are initiated in different ways. In this chapter we will see that there is no uniformity in the practice of the rites of initiation. Even within the Catholic Church we find that there are several different ways of celebrating the sacraments of baptism, confirmation and eucharist. It is helpful to refer to the various methods of initiation as models. We will examine ten such models. It should be noted that the first five actually exist in practice in the Catholic Church whilst the succeeding five are suggestions to breathe new life into these ancient rituals. In order to assess each model on its merits it is necessary to judge them against the criteria delineated in the two previous chapters. The crucial issue is to determine just how effective they are. A rite of initiation that is not effective will incorporate individuals into the Christian community but it won't necessarily make them into the type of Christians who bear the fruit of their new identity. The church is full of validly initiated members but many of them no longer identify with its teachings nor attend the rites of the community. These models, therefore, must be assessed on how fruitful they are in making Christians who continually enter more deeply into the mystery of Christ and his church. They will also be assessed in the light of how they incarnate the dimensions of Christian initiation as presented in the previous chapter.

There are prescriptions in canon law which impinge upon Christian initiation. From the earliest times Christians baptised infants and the church teaches that such baptisms are valid and fruitful. Canon law requires that children born to Catholic families be baptised within a few weeks of birth. Such children should be confirmed when they reach the age of reason, i.e. seven years. But episcopal conferences can decide on a different age (either younger or older) for the celebration of confirmation and, as a result, we find differing practices in various parts of the world. Baptised children, whether or not they have received confirmation, are to be admitted to eucharist at about seven years of age. However, in the case of adults who wish to be initiated into the Catholic Church the practice is different. After sufficient preparation they are admitted to the three sacraments of baptism, confirmation and eucharist in the one ceremony. With these canonical prescriptions in mind let us turn then to the ten models.

1. Confirmation in Late Childhood/Early Adolescence

In this model children are baptised in infancy, admitted to eucharist at seven or eight years of age and are confirmed sometime in late childhood or early adolescence, i.e. between nine and fourteen years of age.

We start with this model because it is very commonly practised throughout the world. Like many of the other models it commences with infant baptism. To begin we will outline this ceremony as it is ordinarily celebrated. The rite of infant baptism normally takes place on a Sunday in the presence of parents, Godparents and a few relatives. The ceremony should begin at the door of the church where all are welcomed, especially parents and Godparents. The celebrant traces the sign of the cross on the forehead of the infant and invites the parents and Godparents to do the same. They then process to the place of the liturgy of the word which is followed by a short homily in which the celebrant explains the significance of what has been heard. The intercessions and the litany of the saints follow this. The anointing before baptism is with the oil of catechumens and the accompanying prayer is the prayer of exorcism. This prayer asks that the child be set free from original sin. The baptismal water is then blessed. The blessing is christological and explains in part the nature of the baptism ritual: 'May all who are buried with Christ in the death of baptism rise also with him to newness of life.' The infant is baptised in the faith of the church and this means that the parents and Godparents profess their own faith and agree to bring the infant up in the practice of the faith. Baptism itself can be by immersion or by the pouring of water on the infant's head in the name of the Father and of the Son and of the Holy Spirit. The infant is then anointed with the chrism of salvation reflecting Christ's own anointing with the words: 'God the Father of our Lord Jesus Christ has freed you from sin, given you a new birth by water and the Holy Spirit, and welcomed you into his holy people. He now anoints you with the chrism of salvation. As Christ was anointed priest, prophet and king, so may you live as a member of his body, sharing everlasting life.' The infant is then clothed with a white garment as a sign of Christian dignity and finally a candle is lit from the Easter candle and the rite finishes around the altar with the Lord's Prayer and the final blessing.

Normally children are admitted to full participation in the eucharist at seven years of age. They then come for episcopal confirmation through anointing and laying on of hands at about twelve years of age. Thus the process of initiation into the Christian community is complete. The advantage of this model is that it is firmly rooted in the tradition of the church and it recognises the role of infancy within the ecclesial community whilst still appreciating the need for a conscious commitment at confirmation. This model also allows for catechesis in preparing for eucharist and confirmation along with a recognition of faith development as the individual is gradually initiated into the community.

The great disadvantage with this model is that it has inherited the unfortunate outcome of the dissolution of the unified rite of initiation that we witnessed in the early church into the three separate rites. Confirmation becomes a truncated ceremony, in many ways devoid of a convincing meaning considering an infant receives the oil of chrism at baptism and thereby can be seen to have already received the gift of the Spirit. Theologians argue that the water ritual of baptism is a Spirit-filled process. The result is that confirmation is searching for a meaning and has become manipulated into the sacrament of Christian maturity or Christian commitment. This can lead to an overly cognitive understanding of faith. Coinciding with this, and perhaps one of the greatest tragedies of this model, is the hijacking of infant baptism in the popular mindset by the doctrine of original sin. As a result it is perceived to be nothing more than a washing away of sin. Due to this minimalist outlook it has become the most private of religious rituals, celebrated amongst a few relatives and friends. There are also serious questions to be asked concerning the role of conversion in this model. Those who see the fruits of the very real conversion process in some of the other models argue that the issue of conversion is becoming marginal in the life of a church that predominantly baptises infants.

The most important issue that must be addressed concerns the fruitfulness of this model. Baptism is the sacrament of faith, not only the faith of the church, but also the candidate's own faith and it is expected that it will be an active faith. Obviously the infant has no active faith and consequently the faith of parents/guardians and of the community must suffice. Infant baptism is valid and will continue to be the norm, yet the clear message emanating today is that those who are baptised should have an active faith. If infants are exempt from this condition then those of eighteen years and twenty years and so on are not. Later on we will see how this model could be recast so as to cater for a more active response to one's Christian identity in later adolescence and adulthood (see models nine and ten). There can be little doubt but that the baptising of infants was a practice of the very early church. According to Hippolytus, 'they shall baptise the little children first. And if they can answer for themselves let them answer. But if they cannot, let their parents answer or someone from the family.' Problems will always remain about the efficacy of infant baptism, problems that the community must come to terms with since it answers for the child. Yet we must tread carefully on this issue because some advocate that only adults should be baptised. This argument demeans the role of childhood and the family in Christianity and turns the church into an elitist community of committed adults. Parents have the right to socialise their children in the faith but this must be done in such a way that truly impacts on the life of the particular individual. It can be argued that an overemphasis on the paschal nature of baptism as conversion can undermine its relevance for infants. The dominant image of baptism in the first three centuries of the church, especially in Syria, was of the Jordan and not of Calvary. The imagery surrounding Jesus' messianic anointing is much more congenial to infant baptism, i.e. divinisation, sanctification, indwelling, power, wisdom and glory. These aspects need to be highlighted during the celebration of the sacrament.

When it comes to first communion and confirmation, is there any sense of changing, of an ordeal of letting go to selfishness in order to be committed to the generosity of Christian living? Where is the ache and the symbols of death that are so integral to initiation? Where is there a real and challenging experience of the sacred, of the spiritual? Where is the encounter with the transcendent, with the sense that we are being initiated into a reality greater than ourselves? A paradigm of Christian initiation must be the upper room on the day of Pentecost. The symbols of initiation saturated the experiences of the apostles who were separated from their beloved master. They had no position nor security as befits those who stand on the threshold. Instead there was an ever present fear and waiting. Their identity as a group, their hopes and promises, had died at Golgotha. It was into this wake room, this place of separation and ordeal that the Holy Spirit was poured forth: 'They were all filled with the Holy Spirit' (Acts 2:40). This is the genesis, the initiation of the church and when we are about the business of initiation it is such an atmosphere that we should do our best to imitate. This and nothing less, for it was in such an experience that the church came into being and it is in such experiences that it will continue to be.

2. Eastern Model

In this model infants receive the sacraments of initiation in one unified ritual soon after birth.

Before we take a look at the tradition in the eastern churches it will be helpful to briefly examine the use of oil in initiation. Traditionally there was a pre-baptismal anointing using the 'oil of catechumens'. It is closely linked with the prayer of exorcism and signifies the care of the church for those who have renounced evil. It is oil that strengthens those who are about to profess their faith. Strictly speaking the oil of catechumens does not seem to be relevant to infants who are clearly not catechumens but because oil is such a rich symbol it can signify the care and protection which the church offers the new born infant. The second oil is the oil of chrism, a perfumed and blessed oil. In the rite of Hippolytus there are two anointings with chrism by the presbyter and the bishop. When the rites broke apart, the western church determined that the first remained with baptism as it does today whilst the second became the privilege of the bishop at confirma-

tion. The baptismal oil of chrism is an oil of thanksgiving because this infant is now united to Christ, the 'anointed one'. It
should be a time of celebration and lavish anointing. Due to
later developments we now associate the gift of the Spirit with
the chrismation at confirmation as the bishop says: 'Be sealed
with the gift of the Holy Spirit.' In the East however a very
different tradition emerged. The Orthodox method of initiation entails baptism, chrismation and eucharist in one ceremony at infancy. The liturgy takes place during Easter and
what is interesting is that the entire ceremony is presided over
by a priest and doesn't include a bishop during chrismation
even though he blesses the chrism oil. It is also quite certain
that the chrismation signifies the presence of the Spirit as the
priest says: 'The seal of the gift of the Spirit.' The outstanding
benefit of this model is the intimate unity of baptism and
chrismation so that effectively there is no perceptible separate
sacrament of confirmation. This is as it was at the beginning
in the Acts of the Apostles and in the rite of Hippolytus. The
unified rites of the East also suggest that when one enters the
paschal life of Christ and the community it is also an entrance
into the life of the Spirit. Unlike infant baptism in the West
chrismation quite definitely confers the Spirit and because
the process is unified confirmation is not delayed until many
years later. One last point is worth noting. Whereas the West
chooses to interpret the meaning of chrism in confirmation in
terms of strengthening and a defence against the world, the
Orthodox tradition connects the odour of the oil of chrism to
the fragrance of Christ and the presence of God. The East
emphasises the beauty and presence of the inner life of the
Spirit whilst the West highlights sin and the perils of the world.

   This model of initiation makes a lot of sense for the infants
of believing parents. Firstly, it nullifies the problem of confirmation, that sacrament which becomes enigmatic in the light
of baptismal chrismation and its references to the life of the

Holy Spirit. Secondly, it affirms infancy as a redeemed state that has its place in the life of the church and God's kingdom. Some commentators highlight the fact that in medieval times childhood was seen as a subhuman, subrational condition. Children were defective adults and therefore the doctrine of original sin rested comfortably with their condition. In response to the reformers and their emphasis on faith the Catholic Church deferred confirmation and eucharist until the child was old enough to profess its own faith but what emerged was an alignment of Christian life with human growth. Those who support the eastern model of initiation can legitimately argue that if an infant can receive baptism in the 'faith of the church' then there is nothing that blocks them from receiving confirmation and eucharist as well.

The problem with this model is of course that it is all completed in infancy. It fails to provide the more mature Christian with any real experience of his/her baptism. So, while it satisfies the theological requirements for initiation, it appears to be rather limited from a psychological or anthropological perspective. As a result it is very unlikely to be applied widely in the Catholic Church.

3. Rite of Christian Initiation of Adults Model (RCIA)

In this model, after a period of preparation, adults become members of the Christian community through the celebration of baptism, confirmation and eucharist in one unified ritual.

Written at the request of the Second Vatican Council, the RCIA was first published in 1973. It is based on the practices of the early church. The period of catechumenate was re-established during which one is introduced into the life of the Christian community. Central to the rite is an understanding of the community as a body that actively accompanies new members into their new Christian identities. The rite states that 'the faithful reflect upon the value of the paschal mystery,

renew their own conversion, and by their example lead the
catechumens to obey the Holy Spirit more generously.' Easter
predominates in the rite and the entire initiation process has a
paschal character. The crucial point to note is that the church
demands that adults be initiated differently from infants. The
three separate rites are dropped in favour of the unified
process of the early church as detailed by Hippolytus. The
RCIA is divided into five sections which we will now examine.

a. Evangelisation and Pre-Catechumenate

This period precedes entry into the catechumenate and is set
aside for the preaching of the gospel and evangelisation in
general. It is a Spirit-filled process during which the candidates are required to mature in faith and they should be
drawn to initial conversion. Like the baptisms in the Jordan
there is an awareness of moving away from sin in order to follow Christ. This is a time when the candidates meet with the
families and communities of Christians along with the catechists, deacons and priests.

b. Catechumenate

Individuals, who have been grounded in the fundamentals of
Christian faith, are admitted into the register of catechumens.
The actual rites of initiation begin here. Repentance, faith
and conversion are the prerequisite characteristics in the life
of the candidate and it is within this rite that the catechumens
are recognised as part of the church though not yet members
of the faithful. Therefore a person begins his or her entry into
the church not through the waters of baptism but through the
actual catechumenate. In order to emphasise the unity of the
rite it is important to realise that the catechumenate is a
Spirit-filled process. One does not wait for the 'sealing' of
confirmation in order to belong to the Spirit. As the Second
Vatican Council taught: 'Catechumens who, moved by the

Holy Spirit, seek with explicit intention to be incorporated into the church are by that very intention joined to her' (*Lumen Gentium* 14).

This is a time of transition and change. Grounded in faith the catechumens leave their old way of life in favour of an incorporation into the Christian paschal mystery. Initiation then is understood not in terms of ritualistic participation but as an active change of outlook and morals. Nor is it an individualistic affair since the rite encourages that the catechumens progress in Christian living with the help of the whole community of the faithful. In a communal context then they live closely with Christians, undergo doctrinal formation, regularly attend public worship and participate in social action of some sort.

c. Period of Purification and Enlightenment

This second stage of initiation takes place during the season of Lent and is marked by a more intense preparation of mind and spirit. It is known as 'election' as the candidates pledge fidelity and write their names in the book of the elect. It is the turning point in the catechumenate, as the catechumens must declare their intention to become Christians before the assembled community, based on their complete conversion of mind and morals. The 'elect' as they are now called, undergo an intense spiritual preparation or purification in the form of scrutinies and presentations. The scrutinies challenge the elect to turn away from sin and the presentations hand on to the candidates the prayers and creed of the church.

d. Sacraments of Initiation

When we examine this part of the rite it is evident that the Council was determined to restore baptism to its Easter setting and also to retrieve the unity of the patristic ritual by initiating the candidate within the tripartite structure of baptism, confirmation and eucharist. Easter is the perfect ecclesial and cosmic moment to situate accurately the meaning of baptism. The dynamics of the paschal event accentuate two realities. Firstly, it highlights in the strongest possible terms, within the liturgical year, the passage of the neophyte into the new life of the Spirit yet only through the painful death of conversion. Secondly, within the setting of springtime and its regenerative powers, Easter is the perfect context for the ongoing process of the birthing of the church of Christ through its new members.

As mentioned before, the rite paves the way for a renewed understanding of sacramental activity within the church. In stark contrast to a cold mechanical approach, the candidates are told that theirs is to be an active faith and they should not receive such a sacrament passively. This is a new sacramental awareness which acknowledges that the sacraments presuppose a committed decision for Christian life. The rite stresses that the newly baptised have entered into a covenant with Christ and such a commitment must be lifelong and dynamic.

Having been accompanied on the journey of faith by members of the local Christian community, the catechumens come before the assembly for the celebration of the three sacraments of initiation together. The ceremony is very similar to that of Hippolytus. Ideally it takes place on Holy Saturday night. At this most solemn gathering, the catechumens are anointed with the oil of exorcism to strengthen their faith in the midst of evil and unbelief. Then they proceed to the baptismal pool or font, where they profess their faith in the Triune God and are immersed or sprinkled three times in the waters of baptism. Emerging from these life-giving waters the newly baptised are anointed with chrism which gives them the fragrance of Christ himself. In this extraordinary prophetic act the church pours the oil of chrism on their heads anointing them with the very Spirit of Jesus Christ. Then the neophytes are brought before the bishop or priest who lays hands on them while invoking the Holy Spirit to come upon them. Finally they participate for the first time in the most intimate mystery of the life of the Christian community as they pray with the faithful, share the kiss of peace and are welcomed to the table for the breaking of bread where they partake of the body and blood of Christ.

The paschal theme runs through much of the baptismal rite as in the blessing of the water and the renunciation of sins. The rite of incorporation into the adopted children of God is accomplished when the candidates profess living faith in the Trinity and in the paschal mystery of Christ. The symbolic death and rising with Christ achieves its full importance with the baptismal immersion and the rite states that this is not merely a ritual of purification but a sacrament of union with Christ. Thus baptism is understood in its truest christological sense.

The rite is quite adamant in restoring the unity of the initiatory process and states that adults are not to be baptised unless they are to receive confirmation immediately afterwards. In this case the post-baptismal anointing is omitted because it is the same as the anointing of confirmation. It is an anointing with chrism and so there is little point in doing it twice. The rite makes a return to the ancient practice of the Roman liturgy as we outlined in the *Apostolic Tradition*: 'This connection signifies the unity of the paschal mystery, the close relationship between the mission of the Son and the pouring out of the Holy Spirit, and the joint celebration of the sacraments by which the Son and the Spirit come with the Father upon those who are baptised' (RCIA no. 34). The culminating point of the initiation process is the sharing of the eucharist with the Christian community. The candidates now enjoy a complete right to participation in this communal ritual. Along with the gathered community they participate in the Lord's Prayer, thus manifesting the spirit of adoption as God's children that they have received in baptism.

e. Period of post-baptismal catechesis or Mystagogia

This is the final stage of initiation and it is felt that having shared in the sacramental life of the community the newly baptised have a greater understanding of the different dimensions of Christianity. What is noteworthy here, though, is the move away from a ritualistic interpretation of the sacraments as it is acknowledged that the symbolic dying and rising with Christ in the baptismal waters, which conversion entails, does not end when the ritual is over. The rite states that what has become important is the personal experience of the sacraments. So here we witness a definite shift in emphasis away from simple validity towards the psychological and more affective experiential fruitfulness of the sacraments. In the ritual much has been brought to consciousness in the individual through the power of symbol and word. But there is also a need to pursue a deeper understanding of what has happened.

In assessing this model of initiation it certainly is the paradigm of what initiation should be about in theological terms. It has a very strong emphasis on the role of the entire community. In the precatechumenate and catechumenate stages it demands a radical conversion based on the gospel and the faith of the community. The RCIA is also characterised by its insistence on the role which faith plays during the whole process. Yet what is outstanding about the RCIA is its ability to facilitate a real transition within the neophytes so that they emerge changed and with a remarkable energy from the process of initiation. This reminds us of the regenerative powers of rites of passage and the transformative powers of rituals of initiation, and so perhaps we can explain the effectiveness of the rite in terms of the dynamics of archaic rituals.

At the beginning of the catechumenate, before the church admits those who intend to become members, the candidates are grounded in the fundamentals of faith and spiritual life. They are required to show evidence of 'initial conversion', a 'desire to change one's life', 'contact with God', a 'sense of re-pentance', 'calling on God' and 'praying' (RCIA no. 15). The subsequent Period of Purification and Enlightenment is 'marked by a *more intense* preparation of heart and spirit' (no. 22; italics added). It is also 'intended to purify minds and hearts by the examination of conscience and by repentance' (no. 25). Finally the scrutinies, 'have a twofold purpose: re-vealing anything that is weak, defective, or sinful in the hearts of the elect, so that it may be healed, and revealing what is up-right, strong, and holy so that it may be strengthened' (no. 25). Without doubt, this is the stuff of the rigours of archaic rituals enacted under the deathly shadow of the ordeals which initiation requires. This doesn't make for pleasant reading and how many of us, baptised as infants, would lament that we have been spared the spiritual chastening of the RCIA? There are celebrations as each stage is completed and there is sup-port for the catechumens from the community, but ultimately initiation must be a self-sacrificial and atrophying experience. If we take the phenomenon of ritual initiation seriously, it must be like this since it is only in the fruitful darkness that transformation can occur. To be initiated means to enter that crucible of transformation where the sacred is encountered. In chapter one we spoke of the 'threshold' and this rite speaks of the progress which the candidate makes through the differ-ent stages as a journey 'as it were, through a gateway' (no. 6). The backdrop to the RCIA is quite definitely that of crossing a threshold, accepting the difficulties of the spiritual journey and experiencing separation in order to leave the past behind and enter a new life.

4. Original Sequence Model

In this model children are baptised as infants and are confirmed at some stage before their admission to eucharist at seven or eight years.

The introduction of the RCIA in the 1970s, with its return to the celebration of the sacraments of initiation in their original order, naturally gave rise to speculation that the original sequence should also be introduced for children. Given the canonical prescriptions outlined earlier, this would demand that confirmation be celebrated before eucharist which would continue to be celebrated at about seven years of age. Thus the original sequence would be re-established, i.e. baptism and confirmation being celebrated before eucharist. The first trend that emerged was to baptise and confirm shortly after birth, followed later by first communion. The great advantage with this was that it placed confirmation in the proper setting of baptism thus restoring the apostolic and patristic traditions. But more attention was given to another structure where infants are baptised but confirmation is deferred until just before first communion at seven years or so. This was thought to be more practicable and children could be prepared for both confirmation and eucharist. This model is becoming popular amongst some liturgists, parents, pastors and bishops. One argument against this model is that confirmation, if it is to be moved, should be reunited with baptism in infancy where chrismation actually occurs in the first place. Such a move would endow the rite of baptism with a much greater emphasis on the Holy Spirit. Or why not drop confirmation altogether? It is arguable that confirmation was the creation of Faustus of Riez, a fifth century French bishop who deemed that it was necessary in order to receive the gifts of the Spirit. The idea took four centuries to catch on and ever since we've been looking for a meaning behind it. Furthermore, confirmation as a separate sacrament simply did not exist in the Apostolic or Patristic churches. We saw this clearly in chapter two. In the Acts of the Apostles (10:44) those who heard the word and received the Spirit were then baptised and there was no confirmation. In the writings of Tertullian and Hippolytus an initiatory continuum existed between baptism and the conferral of the Spirit without a specific sacrament of confirmation. On this basis the argument for proper order is dubious because if confirmation did not exist then how can it be placed into a proper sequence? In the last chapter we also noted how in the Syrian and Armenian liturgies the chrismatic anointing *preceded* immersion, so that it becomes quite impossible to discern anything near a proper sequence from history.

It is difficult to argue that there existed an original sequence in the apostolic or patristic eras. Confirmation didn't exist as a separate sacrament and had no meaning outside baptism, so that the only sequence was baptism/chrismation preceding eucharist. It cannot be argued therefore that baptism *and confirmation* must precede first eucharist in order to be 'original' if confirmation didn't exist when things were 'original'. This model also seems to focus entirely on the role of confirmation as if it bestows some extra spiritual increase and therefore must be catered for before communion and full initiation into the community. The idea that a separate sacrament of confirmation is necessary before eucharist in order to assure a 'fuller initiation' is very questionable. Essentially putting the sacraments in the right order doesn't suffice in reforming the process of initiation, because the problem is far greater than simply one of proper order or sequence. Finally, this model makes no effort to reform the actual rituals of initiation as any problem is seen to lie with sequence as opposed to the efficacy of the rites themselves. In terms of an experience of initiation which might lead to a renewed sense of Christian identity, this model fails to impress.

5. Confirmation in Late Adolescence Model

In this model children are baptised in infancy, admitted to eu-
charist at seven or eight years but confirmation is postponed until
late adolescence, i.e. sixteen to eighteen years of age.

The primitive rituals of transition or rites of passage are
mirrored in the contemporary sacramental life of the church.
There is a perceptible change in a person's identity after, for
example, such rituals as baptism, first communion, marriage
or ordination. The problem with confirmation is that as a
'transition ritual' or rite of passage it is very difficult to perceive any change in the person once the rite is finished. This
model might give some scope to address this issue. One of its
advantages is that it frees confirmation from childhood or
early adolescence. Thus it can become a rite of commitment
later in adolescence. The word itself suggests this: the participants confirm the significance of baptism and eucharist in
their lives and in a very personal way renew their baptismal
promises and membership of the eucharistic community;
similarly the bishop (or the priest) confirms their acceptance
into the Christian community and the Holy Spirit is given to
them to strengthen their commitment to a life of discipleship.
The celebration could become a time for revisiting the potent
symbols of baptism, and the anointing with chrism and laying
on of hands could be done in such a way as to truly affirm
Christian identity. As the word implies, 'confirmation' is a
ratifying of the gifts given at baptism. Simply because baptism is once off doesn't mean that there is no need to revisit it.
Confirmation could be understood in terms of a 'stirring up'
of the neglected or forgotten symbols and meanings of the infant ritual. As the author of the Second Letter to Timothy
said: 'I remind you now to fan into a flame the gift that God
gave you when I laid my hands upon you' (2 Tim 1:6). Given
some imagination and creativity, the baptismal nature of the

sacrament of confirmation could be enhanced. From a cate-chetical and pastoral perspective the renewal of confirmation may be a much simpler and less confusing process if people were not admitted to the sacrament until their late teenage years.

As with all rites postponed until late adolescence, there is an obvious problem – many youngsters may choose not to be confirmed. This poses an important question for the church: which does it desire more – that all children be confirmed or that confirmation become a personally chosen act of commit-ment later in adolescence? Clearly there is legitimate disagree-ment on this issue. Those who argue for the earlier age main-tain that the grace of the sacrament should be denied to no-body; those who prefer a later age believe that the faith of the more mature adolescent must be affirmed and challenged. Here again we have the debate over the role of grace and faith in the sacraments. Given the cultural context in which we find ourselves in western countries, there would appear to be a strong case for postponing confirmation to later adolescence in order to nourish a stronger identity with the Christian community.

6. RCIA Adapted Model

In this proposed model insights are drawn from the RCIA to en-rich the practice of initiation outlined in model one (Confirmation in Late Childhood/Early Adolescence).

Simply because infant baptism may be the norm in a given culture doesn't necessarily mean that the insights of the adult rite become redundant. There are three central characteristics in the theology of the RCIA – community, faith and word. What this model proposes is to apply these pivotal insights of the RCIA to the pastoral practice of infant baptism, admis-sion to eucharist at about seven years and confirmation at about twelve years. The three core principles which emerge from the RCIA to underpin a pastoral theology of initiation might be summarised as follows:

(a) Baptism is primarily a communal rather than an individual affair and so it should only be celebrated in a living community.

(b) Christian initiation is meaningless without faith. In fact it is scandalous to celebrate the three sacraments of initiation in anything but a faith context.

(c) The word should precede the sacrament. People must hear the good news before they celebrate it in ritual.

These principles seem to sit rather strangely with the practice of initiation in many countries. This is especially true of baptism, which often appears to be no more than a family gathering with little emphasis on the Christian community, the fostering of faith or the evangelisation of the participants. To be fair, we did not end up with this type of baptismal situation by accident. It emerged from some of the greatest debates in the history of Christianity.

From earliest times some Christians have had an elitist understanding of the church, that the church is only for the deeply committed and that the less than full blooded should be excluded. These people suggested rebaptism for those who did not live up to the demands of their infant baptism. Others argued that we are not really saved by the grace of baptism but by the type of lives that we lead – if we do not live in a certain moral way then we cannot be saved. This seems to suggest that salvation is as much our doing as it is God's work. In response to these tendencies, Augustine formulated his theology of baptism and his key insights have been accepted by the church ever since: baptism is God's work and so it is gracious, efficacious and irrepeatable. One can formulate three principles to encapsulate the result of these historical arguments over baptism:

(d) Baptism is necessary for salvation.

(e) Since God's Spirit is bestowed in baptism and will never be revoked, then the sacrament cannot be repeated.

(f) Baptism is God's completely free gift and is available to all.

It is interesting to compare principles (d–f) with those of the RCIA (a–c). There is a notable contrast in emphasis: the Augustinian tradition revolves around the grace of baptism and what it does for the individual, whilst the RCIA and most contemporary thought understands an essential aspect of baptism as entry into a living faith community which witnesses to the presence of Christ and the Holy Spirit. The former is based on God's work, the latter on our response to God's work. The two positions are not mutually exclusive but it is instructive to look at what happens if you promote one to the exclusion of the other as has happened in our tradition. If one takes the Augustinian argument to an extreme then one ends up baptising everyone, maybe even those who do not want to be baptised (as certainly happened in the history of the church), for what matters is not human choice but God's grace. If one over-emphasises the faith/response dimension of baptism then one can tend towards suggesting that the church is really a sect or an elite of the committed.

The Catholic Church has traditionally emphasised the 'grace' (d–f above) rather than the 'faith' (a–c above) vision of baptism. As a result, we generally ignore the faith context (or lack of) in which the child will be reared and there is little appreciable role for the community in the baptismal celebration. This model attempts to integrate the riches of these two theologies of baptism in order to facilitate a spirit of deepening renewal and conversion in the church. It also attempts to give due weight to the various issues raised concerning sacramental renewal in chapter one.

In order to retrieve baptism from the private gathering of family and friends, the sacrament could be celebrated with the gathering of the actual community at Sunday eucharist. Even though this would lengthen the liturgy, it would help to overcome the anonymity of baptism by welcoming the new members who now form part of the *ecclesia*. It needn't happen every Sunday and in fact Easter would be an ideal time for baptising, as would Pentecost Sunday. Either way it is important that the community actually welcomes its new members and in many cases it could be a way of actually welcoming a new family into the community. There is a tendency to take for granted that there will continue to be a flood of newly baptised every year and so there is no great need to be overly excited. However, this may not always be the case and if Christian communities begin to decline, the baptism of a new member will in reality be a cause for celebration.

Baptism must take place within the context of faith and in the case of infant baptism the faith which is referred to is that of the parents. One can however coherently argue that only the children of those who practice should be baptised, as there must be a question mark over the faith of those adults who do not share in the celebrations of the community. Infant baptism is intended for the children of believers. The rite presumes faith on the part of the parents and sponsors of the child. What happens if the parents have no intention of raising the child in the practice of the faith as the rite demands? Do we simply ignore this? Quite the most incredible contradiction ensues when the people who are intended to sponsor the child in faith (parents and Godparents) do not practise the faith themselves. If we ignore the faith context then what exactly are we doing: is it a cultural ritual, a rite that takes place inevitably because the child happens to be born in a particular place? Could Christian baptism possibly be reduced to this? What this model proposes is to encourage an active faith in the parents of those infants who are to be baptised. One way of doing this is to introduce a catechumenate for parents which would facilitate them in renewing their own baptismal promises and enable them to sensibly raise their children in a faith environment. If this sounds strange, it is in no way as peculiar as baptising the children of non-believers. Alternatively, a more radical approach would be to discourage those baptisms which amount to socially determined formalities or encourage those who fail to see the value of such a ritual to postpone until a later time. To facilitate this, a rite of welcome would have to be introduced (along the lines of the Rite of Becoming Catechumens in the RCIA) to establish that the children belong to the community of the church even though they are not baptised.

In order to emphasise the paschal significance of Christian initiation this model suggests that the three sacraments of baptism, first communion and confirmation should be celebrated during the Easter season. Ideally, baptism should take place on Easter Sunday, confirmation on Pentecost and first communion on the feast of Corpus Christi. Thus the fifty days between Easter and Pentecost could truly become life-giving days in a particular parish as the energy of the whole community could converge on the formation of new members.

By insisting on the appropriateness of Easter, this model also seeks to address the issue of symbolic minimalism. Nothing corrodes the fruitfulness of ritual like the neglect of symbolic potency and the argument here is that if we want the sacraments of initiation to be a moment of evangelisation then we must allow the symbols to speak. This means that we must be lavish in our use of water, oil, etc. Looking back to the rite of Hippolytus, and primitive ritual in general, one aspect which is at once laudable and enviable is the very extravagance of symbol that this model encourages us to retrieve. Given the possible pastoral significance of this model we will return to it in chapter four.

7. Eucharist in Late Adolescence Model

In this proposed model the person is baptised and confirmed as an infant and then becomes a full member of the Christian community with eucharist in late adolescence. It must be noted that such a proposal would demand a significant change in canon law.

Those who favour the idea of deferring eucharist until later adolescence argue that our present practice is a symptom of 'sacramental intoxication' and our determination to 'sacramentalise' people with four sacraments (including reconciliation) by the time we are twelve years of age. It is questionable whether these rites are really signs of what is happening in the depths of our lives and in our relationship with the community. The thinking behind this model is twofold. Firstly, it restores an explicit pentecostal significance to the ritual of baptism as was the case in the early church. This makes confirmation redundant in later years insofar as it is combined with baptism into the one ritual at infancy. This overcomes the difficulty of confirmation as a dislodged and truncated sacrament of initiation. The second impetus behind this model is partly theological and partly psychological. From a theological perspective faith remains one of the cornerstones of initiation and if we take the RCIA seriously it should be an active faith. In current pastoral practice the question of Christian maturity and commitment is settled by twelve years. This model suggests that the community should not look for such a covenant until the person is about to leave school at seventeen or eighteen years. By this stage they are leaving home and choosing a career, so presumably the individual should also be capable of making a conscious decision based on their own faith as to whether they want to become fully committed members of the Christian community by participating in the eucharistic gathering. If one takes account of the psychological profile of the adolescent, it also becomes apparent that late adolescence is the time ripe for commitment. What is noteworthy here is the sensitivity to the transitions in a person's life. Within this model, and echoing primitive rites of passage, the community provides a ritual to mark the actual transition from school/home to college or employment.

There are difficulties with this approach, not least of which is the possibility that many young people would simply decline the sacrament, especially males who show a distinct lack of interest in religious matters at this age. Furthermore, what are the pastoral implications of young people not being allowed to receive eucharist until they're seventeen? Do they not go to Mass at all? Do they leave after the liturgy of the word? Or do they go to catechetics classes after the homily? Finally, there seems to be a slight irony in the proposal that the rite of full incorporation into the community would coincide with their departure from school, home and often times from the community into which they were born.

8. Full Rites of Initiation
in Late Adolescence/Early Adulthood Model

In this proposed model the three sacraments of initiation (baptism, confirmation and eucharist) are deferred until late adolescence or early adulthood. It must be noted that such change runs contrary to tradition and would demand substantial change in canon law.

The baptism of infants is rejected in this model. Baptism is for believers and only adults can make the fundamental option for faith that is required. Those who accept this argument only celebrate believers' baptism, i.e. the baptism of committed adults. In this perspective the church is the community of the committed and that is the end of the story. Almost all mainstream churches reject this approach as more in keeping with a sect or an elite than a church. Interestingly, it is practitioners of adult baptism who are most inclined towards the practice of rebaptising those already baptised as infants. The Catholic Church is certainly not going to embrace this approach but one should note its inherent attractiveness. No matter what organisation, club, etc, that one belongs to, it is very fulfilling and challenging to work with a committed group. People have always been attracted to deeply committed religious groups for there is a great sense of identity and belonging. This is why many today flock to cults and sects of all forms and the real challenge that these groups pose to the main churches is: can a church which is open to all create a personal sense of identity and belonging?

This model is sometimes referred to as deferred initiation. The demand for an active faith is taken so seriously that it precludes infant baptism although, strictly speaking, initiation would begin at infancy with a rite of incorporation into the community similar to the Rite of Becoming Catechumens in the RCIA. The person receives the full rites of initiation at an appropriate time in late adolescence or early adulthood. The appeal of this model consists in the unity of the rites of initiation reflecting the ancient practice, and also the vision of a believers' or confessing church of committed and mature adults. Like the previous model, this one can be noted for its provision of a ritual during a time of actual transition for most adolescents. Critics of this approach will cite the silence on the place of children as a significant disadvantage.

While many would argue that a confessing church is a necessity for the future, there seems to be a failure to recognise the pastoral difficulty of terminating an almost two thousand year old tradition of baptising infants. The arguments against infant baptism are obvious: it has little support from scripture and it would appear to offend modern sensibilities about the freedom of the individual. But the arguments for are much stronger. Infant baptism is the tradition of the church, east and west, Catholic and Protestant, for centuries. Christians have the right to socialise their children in the faith and if one takes the incarnation seriously then childhood is as important a period of human life as any other. Jesus was born as a child, he didn't appear on the scene as an adult. Furthermore, it is evident from contemporary psychology that childhood is probably the most important time in the life of the individual. Thus it is clear that there are many arguments in favour of infant baptism and it is certainly going to continue. Another objection to this model could be that actual church membership would fall dramatically as the younger generation, disillusioned as they are with the church, would simply opt not to become members. Whilst the idea of postponing all Christian initiation until around eighteen years might appear ideologically attractive to modern western sensibilities, it lacks all coherence in terms of church tradition, psychology and primitive rites of initiation. As a model relevant to the future of the Catholic Church it has little or no merit. For those who believe it does have value, it should be noted that there are Christian communities (Anabaptists, Baptists, Mennonites, the Amish) who practise this form of initiation.

9. Revisiting Baptism and Initiation for Adults Model

In this proposed model children are baptised in infancy, confirmed according to the practice of the local church, and admitted to eucharist at seven or eight years of age. As adults these fully initiated members of the church are invited to revisit the symbols and stories of these childhood rituals.

In Acts 2:37-38 we read that after Peter's speech to the crowd at Pentecost they were 'cut to the heart' and Peter told them to repent and be baptised for the forgiveness of their sins. If we can adopt this as a touchstone for Christian initiation, then the atmosphere of baptism must be one of radical conversion, in the acceptance of the knowledge that the man Jesus of Nazareth is both Lord and Christ. It is the stuff of dying to the old self to emerge reborn in Christ and the Holy Spirit. The RCIA insists through its scrutinies and purifications on complete conversion. This is initiation as it should be: difficult, harsh, uncompromising yet, paradoxically, immensely rewarding. As humans we are called continuously to the process of change and this is accomplished through encountering the symbols of death and resurrection. Baptism offers such symbols, yet the disadvantage with infant baptism is that adults never get a chance to encounter again in a physical manner the waters of transformation and the oils of gladness. Nor does an adult, if baptised in infancy, ever get the chance to witness the unsavoury ache and pain which should form a part of initiation. This was not the case in the early centuries where all the faithful shared in the stringent preparations of the catechumens. This was and should be the real meaning of Lent. The purpose of this model is to facilitate adults in revisiting the symbols of baptism, because those baptised in infancy have no recollection of the ritual and its symbols. Here adults can renew their baptismal promises at Easter, but in a setting and in a manner which is reminiscent of the primitive rituals of initiation. This would facilitate an experience of the initiatory symbols of death and separation. In practice, this model would consist in bringing a group of adults away together to a separate place, removing them from what is familiar, in order to enter the transitionary realm of the sacred. In this holy place various rituals would lead the individual to a sense of the threshold and back to the symbols of oil and water, the crucible of Christian transformation. We will describe such possible rituals in detail in the next chapter.

There are three significant arguments in favour of this model:

1. In primitive religions it was not uncommon for neophytes to be told nothing of the nature of the symbols they encountered. However, on the occasion of the next ritual of

initiation, they returned to examine them. In other words, the process of coming to understand the meaning of one's initiation was slow and it was facilitated by further experiences of the ritual. This correlates with the activities of the early church whereby the faithful constantly revisited the place and symbols of initiation with the catechumens during Lent. This model facilitates such a revisiting and it is notable that the furthering of religious instruction is through contact with the primal symbols and therefore it is not merely an abstract affair of the intellect.

2. It helps those who want a deeper experience of their faith. Such an experience would have to embrace the symbolism of death and new birth. There are many retreat centres and retreat days that facilitate experiences of one's faith. Yet, in tune with the insights of primitive rites, this model provides an experience of the genesis of one's Christian identity through an actual interaction with the core symbols of Christianity.

3. Any innovative developments in the ritual life of the community should begin with the adults, as it is they who must initiate those who want to enter Christian adulthood. Rites of passage into adulthood can only succeed in the interaction between significant adults or elders and the younger members. This model will enable adults to become elders – people who have a sense of the demands and dignity of their identity and a capacity to speak of this to others.

There is one possible serious misunderstanding of this model. It does not amount to rebaptising or reconfirming adults. The validity and significance of the sacraments celebrated in childhood are fully accepted. What this model attempts to achieve is a greater fruitfulness for these sacraments in the lives of adults so that Christians might come to a deeper appreciation of the wonderful gift of their childhood initiation. Its intended goal has much to commend it.

10. Revisiting Initiation with a Rite of Passage
into Christian Adulthood Model

In this proposed model children are baptised in infancy, con-
firmed according to the practice of the local church, and admitted
to eucharist at seven or eight years of age. In late adolescence these
fully initiated members of the church are invited to revisit the
symbols and stories of these childhood rituals.

Looking back over the models proposed thus far, it becomes
apparent that the emphasis is on the timing and ordering of the
sacraments of initiation. Various options regarding the sequence
have been given and for very good reasons. The present model
is based not on when we celebrate the sacraments of initiation,
nor in what order, but on how fruitful they are.

As the name suggests, this model proposes that a new ritual
could be created based along the structure of traditional rites
of passage. In primitive cultures one of the most significant
rites of passage facilitated initiation into adulthood. This
transition was seen as a time appropriate to initiate the individual into the realm of the sacred and to adopt the beliefs and
customs of the group. We know from the primitive material
that these rites were very efficacious. This model proposes
that a rite of passage into Christian adulthood be created so as
to initiate a person into the world of adulthood and the sacred,
using the symbols of baptism. The ritual would revisit the
previous rites of initiation yet provide an opportunity for
young people to actively commit themselves to their community and to the message of Christianity as befits an adult.
Such a ritual would most likely occur at the end of second-
level schooling or soon afterwards. It also endorses the primitive
practice of initiating individuals into society and the spiritual
during their transition into adulthood.

This model does not call into question the initiation that
is already complete. What it does question is the ability of the
sacraments of baptism, confirmation and eucharist celebrated

in childhood to bring about change at the significative level of experience. The true efficacy of a sacrament should be discernible in terms of ecclesial and communal responsibility and service. Put simply, the young person after initiation should be able to signify to the community through his or her life that they are now different in some way and accordingly want to make a different contribution. This model doubts that such a change actually occurs for the individual in a visible ecclesial fashion after the rite of confirmation has ended. What we have learned from the ritual process and the dynamics of rites of passage is that, if the community wants rituals to transform people in a manner that they can experience and appreciate afterwards, as befits initiation, then the rites must occur in a demanding setting. There is a psychological price to be paid if the old self is to die and a new identity to emerge. This model seeks to embellish the sacraments with an initiatory aura. It seeks to provide individuals with a Christian experience, severe as it may be, of transformation and regeneration, death and resurrection.

The challenge is to create rites so that the person can experience, in the nothingness and silence of the threshold period, something of the transformative presence of the divine and the group. It is in the nature of the God of Christianity, the God of Easter, to be revealed in silence, in the wilderness, in non-sense, in paradox. Obviously much effort and imagination is required to construct rituals which could lead people to such epiphanic moments, but the effort becomes even more worthwhile if it can also create a real experience of community. In order to achieve these goals, a certain hardship will have to be endured as a group. Lowliness and homogeneity will foster a sense of a sacred 'community of comrades'. Such bonds mirror in spirit and form the very relationships Jesus enthused about in the gospels. Experiences like these are the foundation of ecclesial community, for it was such deep generic bonds that were fashioned amongst the disciples behind the locked doors of Holy Saturday. The critical issue that we face today is creating a sense of Christian community in which people practise the dimension of real encounter and fraternal love. This model proposes to create the setting which could prove to be the nurturing ground for such a communal reality. In the next chapter we will analyse this in more detail.

CHAPTER FOUR

The Pastoral Application of Three Models

It is the purpose of this chapter to examine in greater detail three models of initiation. The three are number six (RCIA Adapted), number nine (Revisiting Baptism and Initiation for Adults) and number ten (Revisiting Initiation with a Rite of Passage into Christian Adulthood). The reason for the choice of these three is simple. Models one to five actually exist in practice in different parts of the world; the application of models seven and eight would demand substantial change in canon law which is very unlikely to occur, so models six, nine and ten pose the most interesting pastoral possibilities for the renewal of sacramental life in the church. Furthermore, their application raises no canonical problems as a particular parish would continue with its present approach to initiation (in line with one or more of models one to five) and would use all three of these models or some varied combination of them to breathe new life into the existing structure of initiation.

The approach here will be determined more by practicalities than by theological scrutiny as we have already assessed the merits and shortcomings of the various models. It is clear that the RCIA stands as a paradigm of how to incorporate adult members into the Christian community, yet its insights may appear redundant in countries where the vast majority of those who are baptised are infants. The sixth model, the RCIA Adapted, does however offer to retrieve many of the riches of the adult rite and apply them to the dominant pas-

toral model (number one). It is for this reason that it will be
assessed in greater detail here.

Whilst all the models analysed in the previous chapter are
valid rites of initiation, the question remains as to how fruitful
or effective they are. An effective ritual of initiation is one
which makes people into Christians in such a way that they
live their lives in a totally different way than they otherwise
would have. The RCIA applies rigorous standards to those
who wish to follow Christ. Similarly in the rite of Hippolytus
it was not easy to become a Christian. There should be something radical, different and transforming about initiation. Put
simply, something should happen that makes both the individual and the community more aware of what Christian
identity is about. One way that our rites could become more
transformative is by taking on board some of the insights of
primitive rites of initiation. Models nine (Revisiting Baptism
and Initiation for Adults) and ten (Revisiting Initiation with a
Rite of Passage into Christian Adulthood) both apply anthropological insights into ritual to Christian initiation and for
this reason we will describe them in greater detail in this
chapter.

RCIA Adapted Model

The three sacraments of initiation are baptism, confirmation
and eucharist. Through these three rituals one becomes an
initiated member of the Catholic Church. We make the most
extraordinary claims concerning these three rituals. One can
speak of the four-fold effect of baptism: the baptised are immersed in the paschal mystery of the death and resurrection
of Jesus, they become members of the church which is
Christ's body, all sin is washed away and the Spirit of God is
poured into their hearts as they become sharers in the very life
of God. Just read over these again; this is awe-inspiring stuff!
There is no ritual in any tradition that makes such lofty

claims. But do the baptised actually believe all of this? A key problem arises with how the folk experience the sacrament; the manner in which we actually celebrate it undermines the very claims that we make. The ritual of baptism cannot bear all the reality we vest in it. We need to revitalise the celebration so that participants begin to actually encounter the effects in the ritual act. The repetition of words is never sufficient to savour the depths of mystery; only symbol and ritual can touch and taste these broader horizons – that our lives are enfolded in a paschal embrace; that we are not alone but belong to others and the cosmos; that blindness and fear can be overcome, and that divinity has embraced humanity. But even that is not the end of this story, for in confirmation these claims are confirmed and in the eucharist they are incarnated anew as we partake of the body and blood of Christ. Any anthropologist studying the rites of Christian initiation could not but be impressed by the theory behind them. The task of the ecclesial community today is how to allow these ancient rituals speak anew.

How then can we give people a sense of these Christian realities? The RCIA suggests a focus on three key issues – faith, community and word. As we analyse these areas in some detail it is important to remember that parishes vary enormously in terms of the number of those who are to be initiated. This will have significant practical implications for the way the RCIA might be adapted for a particular parish, as the numbers participating in baptism, first communion and confirmation will pose both difficulties and possibilities.

Faith

This model is an attempt to draw on the insights of the RCIA in order to inform and renew the practice of infant baptism, admission to eucharist at about seven years and confirmation later in childhood. One possible strategy was suggested in the last chapter in the original outline of this model – parishes could become much stricter in deciding who to admit to these rites of initiation. The sacraments demand and nourish faith. It is the tradition and law of the church that the sacraments should not be denied to those who ask for them, provided they are properly disposed. This latter point is critical. What does 'properly disposed' mean? In the case of infant baptism it means that there must be a well-founded hope that the child will be reared in the faith. Therefore the disposition of parents/guardians/sponsors is all important. A problem naturally arises in the judgment of this disposition; ultimately responsibility rests on the parish priest though one could conceive of parish structures whereby the community would make the decision concerning who is to be baptised. The strictest interpretation of 'properly disposed' is that the parents/guardians/sponsors must practise the faith themselves. A similar approach might be applied to first communion and eucharist. The other extreme is to admit all those who request these sacraments freely. In this model we are following a middle path between these two extremes. The basic principle of admitting to the sacraments all those who request them is accepted. However, in order to give due weight to the community's (and especially the parish priest's) responsibility of determining proper disposition, it is suggested that the sacraments be celebrated in a way that will foster a sense of faith and identity with the local Christian community. In this way the model attempts to satisfy the two prongs of the law of the church – that the sacraments should be freely given and that those who participate in them should be properly disposed. Thus the sacraments would nourish the faith of those who come to them in faith.

Community

Initiation is a communal rather than an individual affair. No effort should be spared in doing away with any semblance of private baptism. It should never be a private family affair and if it is then this should be changed. A collection of two families from hither and thither does not constitute a gathering of the church. The underlying reason for the 'privatisation' of baptism is that it is perceived in the popular mind as essentially concerned with freeing the individual from original sin while often forgetting the other effects of the sacrament: participation in the paschal mystery, entry into the community of the church and the giving of the Holy Spirit. By right, baptismal celebrations should take place during the key gathering of the local community at its Sunday eucharist. This is not nearly so difficult as many suggest. If the ceremony takes place outside of Sunday Mass then it should only occur in the context of a significant gathering of the community. Of course, if a true communal emphasis is to be introduced then the present 'supermarket' syndrome of shopping around for a suitable priest and/or church must be overcome. Nothing could be more indicative of a privatised notion of baptism than people perceiving it as available on demand. Serious efforts must be made to overcome these gross misunderstandings. There is no pastoral or theological reason why baptism should occur in any context other than a gathering of the local parish community. It is lamentable that in our present situation many rituals of far lesser ecclesial significance occasion a larger assembly of the community than does baptism.

The celebration of first communion and confirmation should also take place during Sunday Mass. The fact that a particular Sunday would have to be set aside for each of these sacraments is a bonus, as it will help the community to focus on the meaning of these rites in the lives of Christians. Since admission to full eucharistic communion is the greatest gift that the Catholic Church can bestow on its members, it is surely fitting that it occur during a Sunday Mass. Parishes

which have large numbers of first communicants might con-
sider offering first communion at any one of several Masses
on the relevant Sunday. In the case of confirmation the gathered
community could pray for its young members as they enter
adolescence and the communal celebration might become a
focus for the adult members to discern ways in which they
could nourish and affirm the faith of the newly confirmed.

Word

To preach the good news of the death and resurrection of the
Lord is the origin and goal of all sacraments, especially baptism. Lent and Easter emerged as liturgical seasons to prepare
for and celebrate baptism. The baptismal liturgies of Lent
make little sense to many people because Lent is seen as a
time of very personal penitential renewal. Valid as abstaining
from foods, cigarettes and alcohol might be, it is hardly the
most potent manner of reminding people of the paschal significance of their baptism. We need to retrieve Lent, Easter
and baptism from the clutches of an all-too-private piety,
which is exactly what the RCIA attempts to do. To give a
proper focus to the paschal character of baptism some suggest
that we should only baptise at the Easter vigil. Though it
sounds extreme such an idea has strong roots. The least that
must be insisted upon is that baptism should occur only on
occasions of paschal significance, i.e. on Sundays. There is no
reason why it should not be limited to some Sundays of particular significance, obviously Easter and Pentecost, maybe
another Sunday during the Easter season while the feast of the
Baptism of Our Lord also suggests itself. Why tie baptism to
certain Sundays? In doing this one can seriously link evangelisation with the sacrament as the very act of explaining why it
occurs on certain occasions would be part of the process of
evangelisation. Nothing so distorts baptism as the idea that it
must be performed immediately lest the child dies and faces

the wrath of God. The very act of postponement until a more suitable liturgical date redresses this inaccuracy and is catechetical in itself because people question the delay. Catechesis works best when it answers questions. The same is true for confirmation and first communion. The obvious Sundays for these celebrations are Pentecost and Corpus Christi.

There are other values associated with this approach. The penitential dimension of Lent could be reaffirmed as a time of preparation for the renewal of one's baptismal promises at Easter. Thus Lent would receive a new focus and a heightened anticipation as the community looks forward to the baptism of significant numbers of infants (and possibly adults) on Holy Saturday night and on Easter Sunday. The Easter vigil is the greatest liturgical ceremony of the year. Its riches are so powerful that it is a pity not to re-enact some of them at Masses on Easter Sunday morning. This model suggests that these Masses be turned into baptismal celebrations where those already baptised are challenged to renew their own baptismal promises while welcoming new members into the community. In busy parishes with many Sunday Masses, it would probably be necessary to reduce the number of celebrations on Easter Sunday morning. Again this has the bonus of awakening everyone to the fact that this Sunday is different, it is the most important day of the year and so we must take more time at our eucharistic gatherings. This might also put an end to the rather silly practice of Masses on Easter Sunday evening. The least we should demand of Catholics is that they attend the Holy Saturday vigil or Mass on Easter Sunday morning; providing alternative celebrations later that day is pandering to the worst forms of consumerism.

The most important advantage of this model is the new energy and drive it would create to preach the word, not through explaining the meaning of Christian initiation, but rather by immersing the people every year in the story that

makes us God's own people, a royal priesthood, a holy nation,
a people set apart. Just look at the possibilities. On the first
Sunday of Lent all of the children to be baptised, admitted to
first communion and confirmed during the up-coming
Easter season could be presented to the community either
personally or through the posting of names and photographs.
Preparing these youngsters and their parents for the relevant
sacrament would become the central goal of all parish activity
over the coming weeks. On each of the Sundays of Lent,
through preaching, drama, mime, dance and even storytelling,
the community could be immersed in the story of baptism in
the death and resurrection of Christ. In anticipation of Holy
Week the parish could organise a penitential service at which
all of us who have been baptised would publicly acknowledge
our failure to live in accord with our baptismal calling. This
might also be an occasion for those who are preparing for first
communion to be admitted to the sacrament of reconciliation. A group of people could travel to the chrism Mass in the
cathedral to join with representatives from every parish in the
diocese at what is the most important diocesan gathering of
the year. The bishop blesses the oils which will be used in the
sacraments of baptism, confirmation, ordination and anointing of the sick during the coming year. At the end of the Mass
the bishop could present these oils to the group from each
parish who would then return to their own church with this
sacred gift. During the evening celebration of the Lord's
Supper on Holy Thursday they could present this gift to the
community and place the various oils in suitably decorated
parts of the sanctuary. On Good Friday and Holy Saturday all
sacramental celebrations are banned as Christians await the
vigil of the Lord. The ceremony on Holy Saturday night
should be the most lavish and joyous of the year. It could
begin with a great fire outside in the darkness. The paschal
candle is lit from this fire and the people follow it into the

church. There they hear the word of God as on no other occasion during the year. Preferably this should not be through simple proclamation as some of the readings could be dramatised or recounted in a storytelling fashion. This would be followed by the highpoint of the year when all present would renew their own baptismal promises and then welcome new members into the community. Those who attended the chrism Mass with the bishop a couple of days before could carry the oil of catechumens and the chrism oil to the parish priest for the celebration of baptism. Afterwards all present could come forward to be blessed individually by the water in which the babies have just been baptised and they could be anointed with the oil of chrism in commemoration of their own baptism. If there are adults to be initiated they are confirmed immediately and then admitted to eucharist. When all of this is complete the babies can be taken home and the community continues with the celebration of the eucharist. If it all leads to a big party afterwards, so much the better!

Easter Sunday morning is like no other. Christians rise to celebrate their greatest festival of the year. Mass on this day should be different; at the very least baptisms should be included at every eucharist on this morning. With a little imagination this could become a day of rich ritual experiences. Parishes with significant hills or mountains might have an early morning celebration on such a hallowed spot. Families could be encouraged to feast on lamb – turkeys and trees have nothing to do with the Christian understanding of Christmas but lamb is inseparable from the story of passover and Easter. The lamb to be eaten at lunch or dinner could be blessed at Mass and during the meal parents could recount to their children the story of the passover and the innocent lamb that was slaughtered. Families might also bring home blessed water and oil from the communal celebration.

The fifty days of Easter would become a time of preparation for confirmation and first communion. During this period attention could be centred on the chrism oil which would have already been used for the recent baptisms and will also play an important role in the upcoming sacrament of confirmation. The preparation for Pentecost could be catechetical for the whole community by reminding people that the Holy Spirit created an assembly of believers rather than a collection of individuals; the various groups working in the parish could make themselves and their work known and call others to put their charisms at the service of the community; those who have endured much (through illness, bereavement, family problems, substance abuse or other issues) and rediscovered their faith in the midst of all this, might bear witness to the presence of Christ and God's Spirit in our midst. But these weeks should be characterised most of all by prayer and support for the youngsters who are to be confirmed. On Pentecost Sunday the laying of hands and the anointing with oil re-enact some of most ancient traditions of the church. Every Mass on this Sunday should include the sacrament of confirmation.

Finally on the feast of Corpus Christi, two weeks later, the community would welcome its seven and eight year old children to the banquet of the eucharist. Ever since Ash Wednesday the parish has been looking forward to this day. Now it can share its greatest gift with another generation. Every Mass on this Sunday (or Thursday) should be a celebration of welcome of children to the eucharistic table for the first time.

Some objections considered

People will raise many questions concerning this model; it's not possible in terms of numbers; what of those who want their child baptised immediately? In reality it is possible: many of parishes have less than twenty baptisms per year, and no parish has so many as rules out the possibility of a proper communal paschal-linked celebration. At any rate the likelihood is that the numbers will fall in many places. The other question is a more serious one. Both the rite and the law require that infants should be baptised within a few weeks. What is proposed here would involve postponing baptism for a short period. With regard to this issue, the model is trying to balance the church's tradition of baptising as soon as possible after birth with the need to foster a proper disposition of faith, to cultivate the involvement of the community and to evangelise all concerned. Of course in the case of emergency children would continue to be baptised immediately. Celebrating baptism only on Holy Saturday night and Easter morning would probably raise canonical problems, so the best policy might be to baptise at Sunday Masses on three other Sundays during the year. The most plausible Sundays are the feast of the Baptism of Our Lord (early January), the sixth Sunday of Easter (normally in May) and some other Sunday in August or September or October (in liturgical ordinary time) which would be chosen on the basis of its link with some public holiday. Linking the celebration of baptism with some major civil holiday makes more sense than one might imagine, as it accords with the church's long tradition of inculturation wherein a non-Christian feast is vested with Christian significance. To remain true to the spirit of this model it would be important for the parish to treat these three days as 'baptism Sundays' so that proper attention could continue to be given to the issues of faith, community and word. Baptism would never be celebrated in the parish apart from these four Sundays except in emergency. In the latter case those who survive their illness should be welcomed formally into the community through the completion of the rite of baptism on one of these four Sundays. Similarly, infants who died before they could be baptised or not long afterwards should be remembered on these Sundays.

With regard to confirmation, there is an obvious objection.

The ordinary minister of confirmation is the bishop, though he may delegate priests to perform the sacrament. Interestingly, the Second Vatican Council (*Lumen Gentium* 26) and the *Catechism of the Catholic Church* (paragraph 1312) describe the bishop as the original minister of confirmation. This echoes the eastern tradition where it is the bishop's blessing of the oils rather than his performance of confirmation that links him to initiation in the parishes of the diocese, and therefore it can be said that the sacrament originates with him. It is also a recognition of the fact that in the case of the RCIA the priest ordinarily confirms the adult immediately after baptism. Undeniably there are advantages associated with episcopal confirmation: it draws attention to the diocesan nature of the church; it is the main reason why a separate rite evolved from baptism, and it provides an opportunity for the bishop to meet parishioners. However, with regard to the latter it is questionable whether confirmation provides the best context for episcopal visitation to a particular parish. There are then two values which this model seeks to balance: on the one hand there is the undoubted desirability of the personal involvement of the bishop in confirmation, while on the other there is the possibility of a new focus on Pentecost as a great festival of the Spirit in the life of the local church. This model opts for the latter.

What the church year might look like
The liturgical calendar evolved as a form of catechesis and celebration which exposed believers in a cyclic way to the central doctrines of the faith. If we applied this model to the life of a parish, it would look like this:

Month	*Season/feast*	*Sacrament*
December	Advent	
	Christmas	
January	The Baptism of Our Lord	Baptism
February/March	Lent	Reconciliation/
		First Confession
April/May	Holy Saturday	Baptism
	Easter Sunday	Baptism
	Sixth Sunday of Easter	Baptism
May/June	Pentecost	Confirmation
	Corpus Christi	First Communion
July/Aug/Sept	Some major public holiday	Baptism
October/November		

Such a calendar would give a new energy and focus to the life of the local Christian community, through integrating the formation of new members with the rhythms of the solar year.

Revisiting Baptism and Initiation for Adults Model

We will examine the rites for adults first, because if a parish were to adopt models nine and ten, the process should begin with adults as it is they who would provide the rites of passage for the younger members in model ten. From the outset, both these models should be taken together as the adult rites provide the setting for the younger members. In the last chapter we saw that these models are based upon the assumption that initiation should be radical, uncompromising and transforming by its very nature. We noted that in the early church the whole community shared in the stringent preparations of the catechumens and thereby revisited the symbols of baptism annually, appreciating anew their meaning and significance. It is also notable that in primitive societies some adults were called to deeper levels of religious experience and they did so by revisiting the symbols of initiation, the symbols of death and new birth.

This model seeks to provide the opportunity of revisiting the Christian symbols of initiation with an adult consciousness. It provides the possibility of reawakening one's Christian identity within the transformative dynamic of ritual and rites of passage. The model will follow a structure of separation, transition and incorporation, meaning that it is based on the theory of being separated from ordinary life in order to experience the power of initiation before returning home.

The model should be seen as being very flexible insofar as any group could plan it whether within a parish setting or diocesan structure or elsewhere. The idea of community may not be so neatly defined as parochial in the future, especially in cities with sprawling housing estates, and this model, as will be shown, provides a compelling blueprint for exactly how to create community amongst people of diverse social backgrounds. What is crucial to the success of this model is the whole sense of separation. This is the idea of pilgrimage, of going away to a sacred place to encounter the reality of life and to be renewed. So too, in the scriptures separation and journey predominate, as after his baptism Jesus was sent into the wilderness, Moses was sent to Horeb where he experienced the burning bush, Jacob was sent to Haran and Jonah was told to go to Ninevah. The destination of such a journey should be well away from home with a very definite sense of separation from what is normal. So forests, mountains, islands and wastelands are ideal. Considering that this model seeks to revisit baptism, a setting close to flowing water is preferable. In accordance with the practices of the early church and the paschal meaning of baptism, Easter is the best time to partake in this ritual.

Before a group sets out it is important to meet beforehand to establish the nature of such a time away. It is not a recreation trip nor an adventure with nature; it has a specific purpose and is uncompromising. If big numbers want to participate there's something wrong. Even though this model caters for adults some elders or leaders should be elected beforehand to insure that they adhere to the rigours of the experience. Elders are also required to facilitate the rituals. This model does not necessarily require a priest to be present.

The very act of going away is an act of separation itself and when people arrive it is best to set up tents, etc. immediately. We noted earlier that this type of time away shouldn't be viewed as simply time with nature yet, having said this, nature plays a very significant role. All primitive peoples understood the cosmos and the natural world as a type of cipher for the truth of life and of the world, yet such a code could only be understood from the religious perspective. These truths were hidden in the rhythms of the natural world yet, significantly, the universe was neither seen as mute nor opaque. The cosmos can be seen as revelatory of the nature of human life. Therefore, like the cosmos, human life should periodically renew itself which is exactly the meaning behind rites of passage and ritual. The notion that interaction with nature or the cosmos on a religious level is the prerogative of eco-warriors or those involved with new ageism is reprehensible. If we are to take the notion of separation seriously we must go to the natural world in order to leave what is familiar behind. Many who have undertaken this model have later recounted that they felt the presence of God in a special way in the rhythms of day and night and in the beauty of the landscape. As Christians we must reclaim with confidence the natural world and take from it an understanding of ourselves and God. The patterns of life and death in our world are profoundly christological and bound up with the paschal mystery of Christ. In Romans 8:22 St Paul tells us that all of creation has been groaning, waiting to be set free, and in 2 Cor 5:17 we read:

'And for anyone who is in Christ, there is a new creation; the old creation has gone, and now the new one is here.'

Here is a possible outline of what might happen when a group withdraws to the threshold of the mountains or forests or uninhabited islands.

Day 1

Arrival in the afternoon.

(a) Set up tents and arrange accommodation.

(b) Work.

(c) Create a sacred circle with twelve stones. This should be big enough for people to walk into.

(d) In the centre of the circle create a square shape with stones. Fill this with a mixture of clay and water. On top of this build a fire.

Rites of Separation

(a) In the evening darken a room and create the shape of a grave using old bones or small stones.

(b) Read an adapted text of Ecclesiastes 3:1-8 as people lie down in this grave.

(c) Reading of a text which encourages people to let go of the past.

(d) Eat a symbolic meal of fish and bread.

(e) Rite of departure into the wilderness.

(f) Anointing with oil. Read John 21:18. Depart to spend the night on one's own in the wilderness.

Day 2

Rites of Transition

(a) After a morning meal gather in a place with running water. Read Genesis 1:2.

(b) People immerse themselves in the water three times.

(c) Use of oil.

(d) In the evening build a threshold and place symbols of the past on it.

(e) Prepare symbolic Passover meal with lamb.

(f) During the meal pass through the threshold.

(g) Destruction and burning of the threshold.

(h) Rite of Accomplishment; separate the fire and jump through it. Read suitable text.

Day 3

Rite of Incorporation

Departure.

Day 1

Preparing the Ground

Using the symbols of the natural world is hard work and so when people have settled themselves in they should be given specific tasks to do. These include the erection of a stone circle, the building of a fire, the preparation of the fish for cooking, the baking of bread, the darkening of an enclosed space like a shed or outhouse (or, if this is not possible, the digging of a shallow grave). There is no discussion about these tasks – people just must do what they are told. Insofar as it is possible, strangers should be put working with each other; nobody should work on his/her own. When these jobs are complete the participants are sent off in daylight to find an isolated place. Each person will erect his/her tent at this location which should be as distant as possible from the stone circle and from one another. Afterwards they should gather just outside the stone circle.

Creating a stone circle is an important task. These stones will create a sacred space, twelve in all with four key stones pointing north, south, east and west. One large stone should be placed in the centre. Like any symbolic action the meanings behind this are multiple but there are key elements. If we look at the first few lines in Genesis we note that after chaos there was order. The primitives believed that creation began from a centre point and it is from here that all life begins and order emerges. The centre point within the circle then is a symbol of the creative process. It can be seen as the place of ultimate possibility. It is the embryonic place of growth. Since ritual concerns transformation, the dying to the old self will be chaotic but the circle represents order and creation. When the circle is complete it is important to create a sense of sacredness about it. In Genesis when Jacob is sent to Haran he awakes from his dream and realises that it is a sacred place. He then took a stone, set it up as a monument, and poured oil on it (Gen 28:10-22). 'Jacob awoke from his sleep and said, "Truly, Yahweh is in this place and I never knew it!" He was afraid and said, "How awe-inspiring this place is! This is nothing less than a house of God; this is the gate of heaven!" Rising early in the morning, Jacob took the stone he had used for his pillow, and set it up as a monument, pouring oil over the top of it"' (Gen 28:16-18). To begin the celebration, the leader tells the story of Jacob and pours oil on each of the stones.

Another feature of ancient ritual was the idea of taking possession of the land by placing order upon it. This can be done by creating a mix of clay and water and placing it within a square of stones around the centre stone. The clay and water symbolise the waters and land of creation whilst the square represents the four directions and the four elements – earth, wind, fire and water. After the centre stone has been anointed, a large fire should be built on top. This circle should become the sacred place for many of the rituals that will be celebrated over the few days as it is steeped in the symbolism of creation and transformation. It is imperative that word and symbol go together. Symbolic action should never be an end in itself. Religious symbols should be transparent and revelatory of the transcendent. An interesting text from Irish mythology for use in the creation of the sacred circle is Amergin taking possession of the land. It is thought to be the earliest poem ever written in Ireland and expresses powerfully a sense of oneness with nature and the spiritual world. It is a poem which is at odds with the loneliness and isolation of modernity and instead manifests a wonderful intimacy with the natural world. This is an extract from it:

> I am the wind which breathes upon the sea,
> I am the wave of the ocean,
> I am a beam of the sun,
> I am the fairest of plants,
> I am the salmon in the water,
> I am a lake in the plain,
> I am a world of knowledge.

Each person should enter the stone circle barefoot and recite a poem such as this. Lastly, it should never be forgotten that this is a Christian ritual and, since baptism is about entering the life of Christ, it is appropriate to link each stage with a corresponding part of Christ's life. A good text to read here is the description of Jesus being driven out into the wilderness (Lk 4:1-12). Like any human Jesus had to go away, to separate himself from the ordinary before he could undertake the ultimate demands of his ministry.

Rites of Separation

One of the key elements of ritual, and especially the revisiting of initiation, is the act of separation. It is part of the rhythm of the natural world that something must die before new life can begin. Rites of separation are therefore crucial in rituals of initiation and there must be something in them of the ache of loss and of letting go. An easy yet effective way of creating a rite of separation is by darkening a room to only candle light. Symbols of death should abound. Bones or candles should be placed at four points to create a rectangle shape on the ground. An elder then should speak from a very real and human perspective of the need to let go in life of all that can hold a person back from moving onwards into a fuller experience of their Christian identity. The following text, or something similar might be used:

> Lord God help me to let go.
> Life is an endless process of letting go;
> In our birth we had to let go of the security of our mother's womb and emerge into a strange world;
> In adolescence we let go of the innocence of childhood;
> All of us have to let go of home, parents must let go of their children and children must let go of their parents;
> Throughout life as we grow and mature we must continually let go of opinions, jobs, good health and ultimately of the idea that we are in control.
> And, of course, in death we must let go of those we love.
> Between womb and tomb life is an endless process of letting go.
> Come, Holy Spirit, help me to let go so that even when the letting go is tearful and sad it will awaken me to the mystery and wonder of life.
> Life is the greatest gift we have received and we must in the end let go of this gift.
> We must let go of the past to let God be the God of the future.

Much can be made here of the need to forgive those who have hurt us in the past or those situations of tragedy and loss which hold us bound in anger and resentment. Absolutely central to baptism in the New Testament was the forgiveness of sins because all relationships must be put right before one can more fully experience the God of Christianity. Each person must become aware of the wounded nature of human life and the sacrificial demands of Easter time.

The scriptural text for this rite can be from any of the passion narratives and it is important that these texts play a central role to stress the paschal nature of this dying in Christ. The shadow of the words of St Paul should envelop this candle lit place: '...when we were baptised in Christ Jesus we were baptised in his death' (Rom 6:3).

One possibility then is to read the text of Ecclesiastes 3:1-8:

> For everything there is a season, and a time for every matter under heaven:
> a time to be born, and a time to die;
> a time to plant, and a time to pluck up what is planted;
> a time to kill, and a time to heal;
> a time to break down, and a time to build up;
> a time to weep, and a time to laugh;
> a time to mourn, and a time to dance;
> a time to throw away stones, and a time to gather stones together;
> a time to embrace, and a time to refrain from embracing;
> a time to seek, and a time to lose;
> a time to keep, and a time to throw away;
> a time to tear, and a time to sew;
> a time to keep silence, and a time to speak;
> a time to love, and a time to hate;
> a time for war, and a time for peace.

After this one by one each individual lies down on the ground within the shape of the grave made by the candles and bones. Another person from the group will then read to them the following text:

> You are not afraid of dying to the old,
> You are not afraid of giving birth to what is new,
> You are not afraid of planting,
> You are not afraid of uprooting what has been planted,
> You are not afraid of searching,

You are not afraid of keeping or throwing away,
You are not afraid of tears or mourning,
You are not afraid of laughter.

Finally it should be noted that some soft singing or humming in the background can be very evocative.

After this ritual the group should gather in the stone circle around the fire. The fire should be large enough to give light and warmth and it should be kept burning brightly all evening. This is a time for preparing the meal and story-telling. The main item on the menu should be fish. A large fish (sufficient for all present) should be cooked on the fire. Bread will play an important role in all meals. Baking it is one of the many tasks that must be completed earlier in the evening. Water and wine should be provided. All sorts of different stories could be recounted around the fire; stories from the particular culture, especially from mythology and folk-lore; stories of personal dreams; stories from the Judaeo-Christian tradition. From the latter the story of Jonah is particularly apposite in terms of his time of separation in the belly of the great fish. Jonah returned from his experience as a very different person. An obvious New Testament story is that of the loaves and fish.

After the meal we prepare to send each individual away on their own into the wilderness. Earlier they will have erected their tents in lonely locations as distant as possible from the stone circle and from one another. The conditions under which primitive initiation occurred were characterised by or-deal and hardship. It is a simple fact that the greater the psychological price paid the greater the sense of accomplishment at the end. Obviously one can't mimic the disturbing ordeals which primitive societies may have employed but the traditional pilgrimage trials of hunger and loneliness can certainly suffice. One of the most meaningful symbols of separation is isolation for a significant amount of time. Great care must be taken when sending people off for a time on their own with little food, yet these are difficulties which can be overcome within the group. Ideally this time of separation from the group should last until the next afternoon (if there were four or five days altogether at least two days would be spent away on one's own). This time away is crucial for a person to yield to the transformative powers of the Spirit. It is within such threshold experiences that the forces of the unconscious and the sacred can fashion inner change and growth. Silence becomes that crucible where a person is forced to look deeply and truthfully at the past, to face the fear of dying to the old, to uproot, to mourn and to throw away that which cannot be part of a more significant Christian future. The participants leave with a rite of departure into the wilderness. Traditionally anointings are associated with strengthening, so all should be anointed before they leave. An appropriate text which can be used during this rite is John 21:18:

> I tell you most solemnly
> when you were young
> you put on your own belt
> and walked where you liked;
> but when you grow old
> you will stretch out your hands,
> and somebody else will put a belt round you
> and take you where you would rather not go.

Other suitable texts are Mark 1:12-13 where we are told how the angels took care of Jesus after he was sent into the wilderness and Genesis 22:14 where, in the story of Abraham and Isaac, we are told that 'On the mountain Yahweh provides'. Like Abraham the participants must trust that the Lord will indeed provide.

The time that people spend alone when they depart to the

wilderness offers an important opportunity for them to reflect on the symbols and actions in which they have participated. These are rich in meaning and they need to be reflected
upon so as to determine their relevance to a particular individual's experience. When they arrive at their tents there are
various rites which they should re-enact for themselves. They
could re-read the story in Genesis 28:10-22 which relates how
Jacob left for the land of Haran. Whilst there alone Jacob
takes a stone and makes it as his pillow. He dreams of a ladder
going from heaven to earth. When he awoke he realised that
God was in the place and that it was sacred. He took the stone
he had used as a pillow and poured oil over it. This monument would mark the presence of God. The individuals can
re-enact this old ritual. It serves several functions. It marks the
place where they will stay as sacred but the actions also tap
into the unconscious and the realm of dreams. This aspect of
the threshold experience should not be underestimated as
many who undertake such rituals relate afterwards the significance of their dreams.

In the morning any dreams should be written down along
with any other thoughts that the person might have. Each
person should be encouraged to record his or her thoughts
and feelings because a threshold time can disturb and energise
the inner life. One of the purposes of this ritual is to allow
change to occur in a person's life and so this can be a time of
transition. One way of acknowledging transition or creation
is by planting something. It could be some bulbs or even a
sapling tree. This action marks the place itself as sacred and
important. Hopefully as the individual grows this will be mirrored in what he or she actually planted. This place can become very symbolic and might be revisited in the future. An
appropriate text that could be used here is the parable of the
sower (Lk 8:4-15).

Day 2
Rites of Transition
There is something about water which is attractive and transformative. Any water ritual must be understood in terms of
the waters of Genesis 1:2: 'Now the earth was a formless void,
there was darkness over the deep, and God's spirit hovered over
the water.' This text is seminal as the waters of the deep in
Genesis become the locus for creation and so they can become a reservoir for the possibility of re-creation. Firstly, water
is indistinct, formless and destructive. In religious terms it
washes away sin and purges the old. However, the second
function of water lies in its creative and regenerative powers.
If one part of us dies a new part is formed. It is therefore in the
dissolution of the formlessness of water that transformation
occurs. In terms of a Christian reading, this is significant because for peoples in all cultures the waters are never intended
to be simply purifying. They also create anew as they are dynamic and life giving. Yet it is only in Easter that water finds its
truest meaning as the dissolution and transformation are finally
defined by the death and resurrection of Jesus Christ.

In this revisiting of the symbols of baptism, the ritual with
water is of utmost significance. The early Christians preferred
running water and in this model a running stream or a river
bank is ideal. This rite should take place on the afternoon that
the participants return from their time alone. The inner path
to transformation is difficult so if the way to the stream is
wild and overgrown it is entirely compatible with the personal
journey. The text from the beginning of Genesis should be
read at this rite along with an account of Jesus' own baptism.
Other texts which are suitable here are narratives from the
flood, the Exodus and Jonah. The participants might first be
asked to dirty their faces and hands with clay and muck from
the ground around them. It is crucially important that each
person immerses his/her head in the waters. There is nothing

more destructive of ritual activity than symbolic minimalism and there can be no place for it here. A suitable text to invite people to the water is from Revelation 22:17: 'Come, let all who are thirsty come, all who want it may have the water of life, and have it free.' The immersion should be triple and at each stage the person can proclaim in turn: 'I believe in the Father, I believe in the Son, I believe in the Spirit.' After the immersion the participants should have a lavish amount of oil poured on them with words similar to, 'You were anointed like Christ, as Priest, Prophet and King. God's favour rests on you.' Ideally the oil should be fragrant with the aroma of the presence of Christ. After this, and in keeping with the tradition of the early church, each person should be given a drink of milk and honey symbolising accomplishment.

Having completed this ritual, the group must set to work on preparing the evening celebration. There is much work to be done; as on the previous day there is no discussion about this – people are just given tasks which they must complete. Insofar as it is possible, strangers should be put working with each other; nobody should work on his/her own. The work that needs doing includes: the erection of a threshold, the building of a fire in the middle of the stone circle, the baking of unleavened bread, the preparation of lamb for cooking.

Passing through the threshold

Later in the evening the group gathers around the fire. The fire should be large enough to give light and warmth and it should be kept burning brightly all evening. A doorway will have been built in the sacred circle in preparation for this evening's ritual. This is a rite of transition and captures in a very physical and spatial manner the dynamic of rites of passage. Anthropologists have demonstrated that social passage often involved an actual physical passage. One of the best examples of this is the passage through a doorway or threshold.

This rite is contextualised by the telling of the story of passover. During this the lintel of the doorway might be painted with red paint. Lamb provides a suitable meal as it links the passover narrative with Christ as the new sacrificial lamb. Different groups can approach this ritual in different ways but the key emphasis should be on leaving the old behind and moving into the new. One idea is to place symbols of the past on the doorway and as each person moves through they can take off an old garment, place it on the doorway and then once they've passed through put on a new garment. During this, the others present might sing or dance or create rythmic noises. As is the case with this entire model, each group can adapt it to their own needs, yet in some symbolic way the idea of passage from one state to the next must be achieved. When each person has passed through the threshold it should be broken into pieces and burnt in the fire. It is then time to deal with the tents. The participants will have brought their tents back with them earlier in the day and they will now be erected in a circle just outside the stone circle.

Everyone should then sit around for a meal of lamb with unleavened bread and red wine. It is important that this entire ritual of passing through the threshold be understood in terms of one's Christian identity. In order to achieve this, those present should be reminded of the story of the earliest Christian believers who spoke of Jesus as the new passover lamb; as the Jews of old were saved by the blood of the lamb, so too we are saved by the blood of Christ, and as the Jews passed over the Red Sea from slavery to freedom, so too we pass through the waters of baptism from our old life of sin to our new life in Christ. Again the words of St Paul should echo throughout the entire evening: 'When we were baptised we went into the tomb with him and joined him in death, so that as Christ was raised from the dead by the Father's glory, we too might live a new life' (Rom 6:4).

Rite of Accomplishment

In paschal terms this final ritual of the evening brings people to an awareness of the resurrection and that the time of dying and of transition must come to an end. Those who have participated in this model will have experienced hardship and loneliness and it is important to ritualise the fact that they have accomplished something worthwhile. Water is a passive symbol insofar as it always seeks to go down, to search for places of lowliness. Fire is an active symbol always seeking expansion and it is also a symbol of accomplishment. A suitable text here is the Pentecost narrative as it reminds us of how the spirit of the new church was heralded in tongues of fire.

This ritual is quite simple yet care must be taken. The fire in the centre of the circle should be separated and each person is required to jump over a piece of it. Before they do so, this is a suitable text to be read aloud and it draws together certain themes. Each person should face towards where the sun has set and raise their right hand in a salute to the universe and say aloud:

> I am the wind of the sea,
> I am the wave of the ocean,
> I am the wind that blows,
> and I am the fire that burns.

> I am not afraid of dying,
> I am not afraid of searching,
> I have gone where I would rather not go,
> and I have drunk from the water of life.

Day 3

Rite of Incorporation

On the day of departure it is important to realise that the experiences which the participants have shared are radically different from that which awaits them in the outside world.

Having spent the few days together some may feel very drawn to their natural surroundings and so may find it difficult to leave. When people are stripped of their rank, status and wealth and placed in an arduous environment, deep generic bonds of friendship can develop. If this occurs then it can be difficult for people to leave a place where they have grown accustomed to and close to others whom they may or may not have met before. A rite of incorporation then eases all those involved back into the familiar world of home, work, family and friends.

This ritual can take place within the context of a eucharist or independently. Obviously this will depend on whether there is a priest present or not; if it is a Sunday morning it is particularly suitable to incorporate this rite in a Mass. The day begins with some breakfast after which the tents are taken down and prepared for departure. Each person is then asked to go for a short walk (thirty minutes or so) alone and to bring back some symbol which speaks to him/her about these few days.

The folk gather in the stone circle around the fire. It is quite likely that some of the embers will still be alight; the fire may be stoked and some small pieces of wood, etc. added, but it must not be made into a great fire like the previous two evenings since it is nearly time to go home. There are three parts to the ritual, namely word, faith and community. If this celebration is incorporated in a Mass, the first part (word) will form part of the liturgy of the word, the second element (faith) will take the place of the homily, creed and prayers of the faithful, whilst the third section (community) will occur after communion and include the final blessing.

(a) Word
The intention of this part of the ritual is to intertwine the story of each individual present with that of the scriptures.

For this purpose, text seven from Appendix Two (My story
with biblical eyes) should be read. After this the leader takes a
large bible and holds it wide open over the head of each participant and says: 'God's word has been sown in your heart;
you are God's word to the world.'

(b) Faith

A text reflecting on the nature of life as journey is read; this
could be Luke's account of the disciples on the road to
Emmaus. After this the leader asks all present to present their
symbols. As individuals speak of the meaning or story behind
their symbols, they will inevitably tell something of what has
happened to them over the few days. As much time as needs
be must be devoted to this part of the ritual. While the leader
blesses the symbols with water, the group sings a song with
the theme of 'journey', or there is instrumental music.

(c) Community

To finish, all the participants are asked to take their personal
symbols and stand in the outer circle of stones. As they face
inwards towards the fire, the text of 1 Cor 12:4-27 is read.
They are then told to turn around and face away from the circle. The priest, or if there is no priest the elder of the gathering, blesses all present in these or similar words:

> You are the salt of the earth,
> you are the light of the world,
> together we are the body of Christ.
> As a baby you were baptised in Christ,
> at seven years you were invited to eat from the altar of God,
> and later the church confirmed the gift of God's Spirit
> given to you.
> Go now from this holy place,
> treasure in your heart the wonder of who you are

and may the words you have heard here ever echo in your mind.

You are the salt of the earth,

you are the light of the world,

together we are the body of Christ.

After this everyone departs immediately. The group might meet again many months later and/or the participants could be asked to write down their reflections on what happened during these days.

Revisiting Initiation with a Rite of Passage into Christian Adulthood Model

This model relies heavily on the tradition of rites of passage in primitive societies. This is a world where the process of death and renewal occur constantly and this is also true of the patterns of human growth. In primitive tribes it was acknowledged that a person must go through different stages of growth and change in order to enter the next stage of life. The passages in life range from birth to childhood, from childhood to adulthood and from there to marriage, parenthood, old age and death. The key to understanding the dynamic in rites of passage is that as humans we are constantly called to change and regeneration. Whilst a mechanical or cosmic system runs indefinitely, human and biological systems need to be regenerated at significant times in a person's life. The curse of the modern world is the breakdown of cohesive communities which, in traditional societies, carried people through these changes in life with the aid of rites of passage.

One of the key transitions in life which every person must go through is the passage from childhood through adolescence into adulthood. Adulthood is characterised by responsibility to family and community. It is characterised by work and a selflessness for others which family and community life

demand. If adolescents are not properly initiated into adulthood, these qualities may not be forthcoming. What rites of
passage provide is significant elders and a community setting
which welcomes young people into adulthood and provides
them with the wisdom and skills to adequately carry out their
new status. Another term for this process is socialisation or
the incorporation of our young people into society. If socialisation breaks down the results are catastrophic for society. One
only has to think of the groups of young people in our towns
and cities who by their actions work completely against the
common good. Robert Bly has written recently on this very
breakdown in American society. He claims that up until the
1950s socialisation amongst young males remained relatively
steadfast but that between 1950 and 1979 the level of serious
crime committed by those between thirteen and twenty four,
according to FBI records, has risen by eleven thousand per
cent. Bly argues that this is due to the failure of socialisation
and in particular initiation. He cites the example of New
Guinea, where initiation practices are declining and for the
first time there are reports of gangs of young men roving the
countryside. Every society bemoans the rise in juvenile crime
and delinquency, but what's interesting in Bly's work is the
link he establishes between social disintegration and the
breakdown in rites of initiation.

If we take such comments seriously, a convincing link begins to emerge between the needs of society in terms of socialisation and the initiatory practices of the Christian community.
It would appear that when we are about the business of
Christian initiation and Christian rites of passage, the ambit
of their efficacy may be more far reaching than we might originally have thought. Christian initiation, or the initiatory
practices of any religion for that matter, would seem to be intimately linked to the very secular necessity of socialisation.
Whatever about the arguments for a separation of church and

state, it would seem unwise to condemn as nonsense and irrelevant those religious rituals that strive to confer communal
identity. One of the contemporary roles of the church may
well be to serve the needs of a society that is illiterate in the
grammar of ritual and initiatory rites. Of all the social institutions, it is the Catholic Church which is competent in ritual,
and of all times, it is the modern era that begs such a profic-
iency.

The rite of passage which this model proposes serves two
needs. Firstly, society in general is in need of a way of socialis-
ing its young people. Secondly, and more pertinent to this
work, in primitive communities rites of passage into adulthood were perceived as the time when a person was initiated
into the world of the sacred. Of all passages this was the one
which had the greatest religious significance.

Before this model could be introduced in a parish, much
preparatory work must be done. It is crucial that there exists
within the community trusted elders who are willing to bring
some of their young people into the state of Christian adulthood. These people should have meditated for themselves on
what Christian adulthood means and, obviously, an ideal way
of doing this is to implement the ninth model on revisiting
the symbols of baptism for adults. An important aspect of this
particular model is that all energy must first be put into estab-
lishing a group of adults who are willing to work with the
young people. Once this is done, the community itself must
be made aware of the process that is about to begin in their
parish. Essentially some young people (there may be only a
very small number) want to become more involved in the life
of the parish community or they simply want to explore in a
deeper way their Christian faith.

The ideal time for this model to be implemented is when
the young person is actually leaving home or has left home for
university or employment. The nature of childhood is that a

person is dependent on their parents so it is pointless telling somebody they're an adult if they have to return home and live off their parents. Parents have to be informed of exactly what is happening to their son or daughter so that after the rites are finished they will in some way treat them differently. The same applies to the community. New responsibilities or ministries must be found for those who undertake this model so that the person will be treated like an adult within their own group.

The structure of the time away follows that of the adult rites. The way to initiate someone further into their faith and their religious identity is by revisiting the symbols of initiation, yet when this is accomplished using the dynamic of rites of passage it should lead to an experiential efficacy that other rites lack. Put simply, when people encounter the symbols of their baptism within a ritual environment, it is an experience that should impact upon them in a powerful way. Four days should ideally be set aside for these rites and the structure of the ritual should follow the same pattern as model nine. The main difference between models nine and ten is based on the nature of the texts used.

The rite of separation needn't take place in a darkened room. The emphasis in this case should be on the departure of the young person from childhood ways. The child is dependant and is not required to be responsible. Nobody looks for wise words from a child; rarely is courage, support and help expected from them in times of crisis. The demands of adult life must be placed before these adolescents but in a manner that is supportive and encouraging. The following text is adapted from the adult rite and can be used in its place:

> You are not afraid of dying to childhood ways,
> You are not afraid of giving birth to wisdom and courage,
> You are not afraid of planting responsibility in your life,

You are not afraid of uprooting childish ways,
You are not afraid of searching for the man/woman that is within you,
You are not afraid of becoming independent and free,
You are not afraid of mourning your break with the past,
You are not afraid of embracing the future.

The rite of transition using the threshold can also be adapted for use with adolescents. When the young people are sent away they can be encouraged to think about what it means in their own experience to break with childhood ways. After the threshold is built they should place symbols of childhood on the frame so as later they can be destroyed. A suitable text that can be read by one of the elders, as the young person approaches the threshold, is from John 21:18.

I tell you most solemnly
when you were young
you put on your own belt
and walked where you liked;
but when you grow old
you will stretch out your hands,
and somebody else will put a belt round you
and take you where you would rather not go.

It is important after this ordeal and experience that the young adults who emerge from the actual physical threshold be given some symbol of accomplishment. They must also be told that the Christian community now acknowledges that they are adults and are invited to partake as such in the life of the community. It is up to each community to imagine how best to incorporate these young adults into its life and work.

In planning for this model, it must be remembered that youngsters in late adolescence do not have the same reflective capacities as more mature adults. This is not due to any emotional or intellectual inferiority but simply results from the fact that they have not experienced life to the same degree. Therefore they may not be able for long spells of time without the company of others. It may, therefore, be wise to erect the tents on the first evening in the vicinity of the stone circle. On the second morning, instead of spending a prolonged period isolated from the group, all of the participants might go on a long trek together, ideally to a nearby mountain top. What is most important is that all three days be physically demanding, as it is in the encounter with the beauty and harshness of the earth that a sense of community can be recreated, and it is only in a living community that the meaning of Christian initiation can be retrieved.

Being able to cope on one's own and cherishing one's own value is a measure of the transition from adolescence to adulthood. Since this is the very transition that the model intends to facilitate, it should not be presumed that it has already occurred. For this model to achieve its goals it is crucially important that there are adults present to journey with the adolescents. Through walking and talking, through eating and drinking, through bearing the hardship together, these youngsters encounter their elders in a new way. This is one of the arguments for organising this model separately for males and females as there is little doubt but that young men and women need the witness of elders of their own gender if they are to grow in Christian faith.

CHAPTER FIVE

The Sunday Mass

The most important pastoral setting in the Catholic Church is the Sunday Mass. During this gathering Catholics are invited to partake in the most intimate reality of their faith – the body and blood of Christ. To be admitted to the table of the Lord is the goal of Christian initiation. Given that our focus in this book is the renewal of the sacraments of initiation we must now turn our attention to the regular Sunday Mass. Its great strength is that it actually exists as a gathering of the community so it naturally suggests itself as a context for reflection and renewal. The first step that needs to be taken is a serious effort to expose members of the community to the dominant trends in contemporary theology of the eucharist. This is probably best done during the actual Sunday Mass because if placed in another context (like a mid-week meeting) it will only touch a few. Again it will demand the use of the imagination to communicate through preaching, reading, music, song, symbol and story. There are different themes that need to be highlighted. We have isolated six that are particularly significant.

1. The Different Names for the Mass

Just to peruse the various titles that Christians have used to describe their central ritual is interesting in itself. Initially it was called the *breaking of bread* since it was at a Jewish meal that Jesus blessed and broke the bread – similarly the early Jewish followers of Jesus gathered to break the bread and share it with one another. The term *eucharist* means thanks-giving – Christians give thanks to God for the wonderful gift of creation and the still greater gift of Christ himself. The *Lord's Supper* recalls the fact that it was during supper with his disciples that Jesus offered them his body and blood. The *holy sacrifice* emphasises the link of this supper to Calvary where Christ sacrificed himself for us. It is called the *liturgy* because it is a public action in which the works of God are celebrated and commemorated. It is an act of *worship* for we bow down before our creator and redeemer and give praise to God alone. And, of course, we call it the *Mass* because it concludes with a sending forth of the congregation to incarnate in their lives what they have celebrated in church. These titles summarise much of the church's faith concerning the Mass.

At a Sunday Mass much could be made of these different names. Over seven successive Sundays the community could be introduced to each one in turn. Their significance could be explored through homilies, commentaries, posters, role-plays and reflections.

2. The Presence of Christ

The Second Vatican Council spoke of the four-fold presence of Christ in the Mass. Christ is present in the assembly, in the word, in the ministers and under the appearance of bread and wine. Let us reflect a little on each of these.

The most important fact in Christian history is that the sad group of followers who scattered on Good Friday gathered again in the light of Easter. The power of God's Holy Spirit brought them together and sowed the seed of faith in the resurrection. Before long the early community was referring to itself as the body of Christ. The Spirit of Christ was present amongst the believers and was poured into their hearts through baptism. So they spoke of themselves as the assembly of God, as God's own people. Today when we gather we too are the assembly of God, we too are God's own people. It is only right then that, when we assemble for our central ritual at Sunday Mass, we should speak of the presence of Christ in our assembly. However small or disorganised, however poor or comfortable, however strong or weak, however traditional or prophetic, when there are at least two or three gathered in the Lord's name the presence of Christ is incarnated anew in the world.

One of the happiest consequences of the Second Vatican Council is a renewed emphasis on the treasures of the scriptures. Slowly but surely Catholics are rediscovering the power of God's word, especially through personal prayer, reflection and study. But it is in the proclamation of the scriptures at Mass, where the assembly is gathered in faith, that Christ's presence should be most clearly expressed. The homily is intended to interpret the scriptures for the particular community and then the assembly responds by professing its faith and interceding for the church and the world.

There has always been a rich understanding of the nature of the priesthood in the Catholic Church. The ordained priest has the crucial role in the Mass as he is the one who presides over the assembly, interprets the scriptures for the particular community and calls the Holy Spirit upon the bread and wine. Through this ordained ministry Christ is present to the community of believers. The other ministries are also expressions of the presence of Christ: the cantors lead the assembly in singing God's praises, the lectors proclaim God's word, the acolytes serve at God's altar and the extraordinary ministers of the eucharist feed God's people with Christ's body and blood and bring communion to the sick and house bound of the parish.

It is, of course, under the appearance of bread and wine that we encounter the apex of Christ's presence in the Mass. Through the words and actions of the priest and the power of the Holy Spirit, the bread and wine become the body and blood of Christ. No other church or religion makes so strong a claim – that we actually share in the very life of God. This is an awe-inspiring belief and so it naturally led to the species being treated with great reverence. The ultimate act of faith for a Catholic is to share in this holy communion.

It is an important task of the church to awaken its members to a sense of this four-fold presence of Christ. There are many practical steps that can be taken to enhance this endeavour.

The assembly

Nothing corrodes a sense of belonging to a particular assembly more than being scattered around a large church building. If there is only a small number of people in attendance they should be invited to gather at the front, close to the altar, or else an alternative space should be created for such smaller occasions. In building new churches or redesigning existing ones, serious efforts should be made to create a sense of belonging to a community. This is why many churches are now circular or semi-circular, and why some altars have been moved to a more central location; why seating is sometimes rearranged in a traditional choir style. In the design of smaller churches and oratories there is a strong argument for not fixing heavy seating to the floor permanently so that the seating arrangement can be varied depending on the size of the gathering. From the Council of Trent (1560s) to the Second Vatican Council (1960s) churches were designed on the premise that only one thing really mattered – the focus on the altar and the tabernacle. Today we need to give due attention to the significance of the assembly which gathers to partake of that which it already is – the body of Christ. Other simple measures which might facilitate a renewed sense of communal identity could include: occasionally inviting people to speak to one another at the beginning of Mass or after the homily; offering some refreshments so that people might linger for a while at the end of Mass, and providing a lot of local information on billboards and posters at some location in the church. This might include projects on some aspect of the history or life of the local community.

The word

The proclamation of the word has improved immensely in many parishes in recent years. Lectors need to be trained and given a sense of the importance of the reading of the scriptures at Mass. Furthermore, their ministry should be recognised and cherished by the community. It is obvious that some people have the charism of being good public speakers while many others do not; clearly it is the former who should be invited to proclaim the scriptures. If the word is not heard then it might as well not have been proclaimed at all – there is no reason today not to have a good amplification system in place. But, of course, there are deeper problems than these. The first reading from the Old Testament is often unintelligible without some introductory words; this need not turn into a homily as a few sentences will suffice. Then there is the contorted question of the merit or otherwise of leaflets which allow the congregation to read the text. The arguments for and against this have been well rehearsed and it remains an open question, but one must remember that we live in a television age where people's capacity to give full attention to a purely verbal communication has been drastically reduced. Nobody needs to be more aware of this than the homilist. It is quite amazing that so many homilies are still so long. Listening to a sermon is not intended to be a penitential exercise but an invitation to explore God's word in such a way that a dialogue is initiated in the listener between the scriptures and his/her own life. Length adds nothing to this; it is difficult to understand why a normal homily should last more than five minutes. If it does then it will be critical to use role play or story or visual image to maintain attention. Unquestionably the key requirement is a serious level of self-reflection in the life of the homilist as it is this which will most likely echo in the listener.

The ministers

Priests badly need affirmation and challenge from their communities. They need to be affirmed in their ministry as leaders, presiders and preachers and challenged to conform their lives ever more closely to that of Christ whom they represent in a special way at Mass. This latter task is extremely difficult as the priest must foster a sense of community in the assembly, interpret the scriptures and lead the eucharistic prayer. The great temptation for the priest is to think that he is on his own and then to lapse into either frustration (where nothing gets done) or dictatorship (where virtually everyone gets alienated). Instead he must cultivate a sense of shared responsibility with the other ministers – cantors, lectors, acolytes and ministers of the eucharist – so that the celebration becomes an expression of the faith of the whole community. The greatest occupational hazard for priests is the repetition of Masses, as familiarity is always in danger of breeding contempt. Ideally a priest should preside at only one Mass on a Sunday. The multiplication of Sunday Masses, except in cases where numbers absolutely demand it, is a very questionable pastoral policy for it splinters the community and fosters a consumerist mentality among the faithful.

The body and blood of Christ

The supreme encounter with Christ in the Mass is to partake of his body and blood in holy communion. Traditionally this is the only form of Christ's presence that was really highlighted.

As a result we have inherited an impressive array of practices from medieval and tridentine times which cultivate reverence for Christ's real presence: genuflection before the tabernacle, bell ringing at the consecration, kneeling during certain parts of the Mass and processions on the feast of Corpus Christi. We even began to speak of the 'most blessed sacrament', for this sacrament was more sacred than the other six. In fact the church placed such an emphasis on the holiness of the eucharist and our unworthiness to receive it that few people actually did so. It was only with the reforms of Pope Pius X at the beginning of this century (see chapter two) that large numbers began to receive communion again. But still great reverence was shown for the eucharist as those who received the host would not chew it but rather let it slip down their throats, and it could only be received on the tongue for ordinary people could not possibly touch something so sacred with their hands.

Given these impressive traditions of respect for the real presence of Christ in the eucharist, it is not surprising that some believers might find more recent reforms and emphases distasteful. But this is unfortunate as they are intended to awaken our appreciation of Christ's presence in its four-fold dimensions. In order to understand the presence of Christ under the appearance of bread and wine in the broader context of the assembly, the word and the ministers, due care should be taken with the following issues.

(i) It is preferable that communion should be received under both kinds as this clearly accords with the way that the eucharist was instituted in the gospels. Similarly, reception of the host in the hand rather than on the tongue is more in line with the tradition of the scriptures and the early church. Obviously nobody should be forced to embrace these habits but it should be clear to all that they are in fact part of a very ancient tradition. No member of the faithful, ordained or

non-ordained, is worthy to handle or receive the body and
blood of Christ, but notice the words we say before communion: 'Lord I am not worthy to receive you, but only say the
word and I shall be healed'. God's word is indeed spoken at
every Mass in the readings from scripture and it is a word of
forgiveness and healing. Difficult as it is to believe, we, with
all our sinfulness and limitations, are Christ's body and when
we come to Mass we are invited to partake of that which we already are – the body of Christ. As we show due reverence for
Christ's presence under the appearance of bread and wine, we
should also cultivate a deep respect for his presence in the assembly of believers. There are two different and important meanings of communion in the church: there is the communion of
Christ's body and blood which we receive in the Mass, but
there is also the communion created amongst those who partake of the bread and wine.

There are other less significant issues which might be addressed in this context. On receiving their first communion
children could be required to receive the host on the tongue
and not allowed to partake of the cup. This would continue
to be the case until their confirmation (presuming that it
comes sometime later) when the newly confirmed would be
allowed to receive the host in the hand and to drink from the
cup. Such an approach would also begin to deal with the
problem that confirmation doesn't bestow any new visible
rights on those who receive it.

(ii) Bread and wine are indispensable to the Mass. The
more obvious it is that we are using real bread and real wine
the better. Since the bread is unleavened it will not bear an
exact resemblance to what we normally eat in our homes but
it should have the texture of bread. Similarly, ordinary wine
made from grapes should be used. If people perceive that it is
common bread and wine that become the body and blood of
Christ then they will grow in appreciation of the meaning of

this extraordinary event – that God's Spirit is transforming our ordinary world into something divine. The original name for the Mass was the breaking of bread. Today the bread is broken after the sign of peace and before communion. This crucial action gets very little attention, not least because many priests break a host and then consume it all. Surely the meaning of the action of breaking is that what is broken should be shared. This could be facilitated by the use of a larger bread which could be broken into many different pieces and then shared in holy communion. The habit of the priest having one larger bread for himself whilst there are smaller hosts for everybody else is rather unfortunate as it empties the action of the breaking of bread of much of its significance. Surely it would be better, especially when there is a small congregation, if there was one bread that was broken into many parts. This would draw together two dimensions of Christ's presence in the Mass as the assembly would share in the one bread and the one cup.

(iii) The reservation of consecrated breads in the tabernacle is an ancient tradition of the church. The original reason for keeping hosts after Mass had ended was to bring them to the sick and others who could not attend the communal gathering. As time went on the practice of prayer before the blessed sacrament developed and this led later to exposition and benediction. A key reason for maintaining the tradition of reservation in the tabernacle is to have communion for the sick and house bound. It should be noted that the reason for the existence of eucharistic ministers is not just to help in the distribution of communion during Mass but also to bring the body of Christ to the sick and house bound. This is a much more enriching foundation for this ministry. A small number of hosts should be reserved in the tabernacle but it should not ordinarily be used as a source for communion at Mass. Ideally, the right amount of bread should be consecrated at a particular Mass for those who wish to receive communion. There is no sound theological or pastoral argument for the reservation of large numbers of hosts.

Personal prayer before the reserved blessed sacrament is an edifying tradition in the Catholic Church. Efforts should be made to link this form of Christ's presence to the other dimensions of the eucharist – the assembly, the word and the ministers. Clearly, if an individual visits a church on his/her own there is no assembly present, the scriptures might not be read and there is no ministerial aspect. But we should encourage those who spend either a long or a short time praying before the blessed sacrament to intercede for the Christian community, especially for those who suffer at this time – the poor, the lonely, the sick, the bereaved, the fearful, the abused. This ties one's private prayer intimately to the life of the broader community. Similarly we should promote the idea of reading and reflecting on the scriptures in this quiet environment; this could be facilitated by making bibles easily available. Finally, those who come before the Lord present in the tabernacle should pray for all of those who exercise a ministry in the church – that they might be affirmed and strengthened in their service of the community. In this way the enduring presence of Christ in the tabernacle is integrated with the gathering for Sunday Mass. However, there should not be any doubt but that the most expressive form of Christ's presence is found in the Sunday Mass where all four dimensions are manifest and encountered. That is why it is true to say that the basic purpose of the church building is to provide a setting for the Sunday celebration rather than a context for personal prayer. This has led to serious disagreements in some communities when efforts were made to move the tabernacle to the side or into a separate space adjoining the church. There is much to be said in favour of this as the main focus of the church building should not be the tabernacle but the altar, the lectern and the presider's chair, whilst a small, warm and comfortable space might more befit personal prayer before the blessed sacrament.

3. Sacrifice or Meal

Sacrifice is one of the defining aspects of all religions. The priest is the one who offers the sacrifice, the altar is the place where the offering is made and the victim is that which is offered. In ancient pagan religions the first-born was sacrificed to the gods – originally this was a human, later an animal or the first fruits of the harvest. During the sacrifice, that which was offered up to the gods was destroyed through being slaughtered or burned. In Christianity all of this changes. In the Letter to the Hebrews there is an extended treatment of the meaning of religious sacrifice in the light of Christ's death on the cross. Christ is spoken of as the priest and the victim for he sacrificed his own life on a new altar – the cross. Therefore, Christians came to understand Christ as the new high priest, the one who offers the sacrifice, but also as the victim, for he was the one who was offered on the cross which became the altar. Thus the ancient tradition of sacrifice is given a new interpretation – the demand for self-sacrifice.

Is the Mass a sacrifice? There is only one sacrifice of Christ, that which occurred on Calvary almost two thousand years ago. But that event is so important that its effects have flowed through human history ever since. From the earliest times Christians began to believe that as they broke the bread and poured the cup they encountered again the meaning and the effect of Christ's self-sacrifice on the cross. Later we would speak of the sacrifice of the Mass – that as we share in Christ's body and blood we are partaking in the fruits of his self-giving for our salvation. So the Mass is indeed a sacrifice, not in the traditional pagan sense of an offering made to placate the angry gods but in the true Christian sense of our sharing in the fruits of Christ's self-sacrifice. In response to this we are asked to sacrifice ourselves as disciples of the Lord.

The Mass is also a meal. As its roots can be traced to Good Friday, so too they can be traced to the last supper of Holy Thursday. On that night Jesus shared a meal with his disciples during which he spoke of the broken bread as his body and the red wine as his blood, and he told them to do this in his memory. The crucial question is what is 'this'? Clearly it refers to the disciples gathering to share bread and wine in his memory, but it also means that we must pour out our lives in his memory, that we must wash one another's feet in his memory, that we must ultimately die in his memory. The Mass is indeed a meal but one that leads to sacrifice, especially self-sacrifice. The origins of the Mass are found in the meal of Holy Thursday night but its full significance is discovered only in the self-sacrifice of Good Friday. As the last supper led to Calvary so must the table of the Mass become an altar of sacrifice, the community must become priestly, the celebration must become an offering and the communion must lead to commitment.

There are many pastoral consequences that flow from an understanding of the Mass as both meal and sacrifice. As a meal it should be a celebration at which all members of the community feel welcome irrespective of social status, racial origin, political outlook or nationality. Though we come from many different backgrounds we share the one bread and the one cup. As a sacrifice the Mass demands that we give of ourselves. The offertory is a good focus for this. Any gifts that are offered, along with the bread and wine, should not be returned; the whole point of this action is that we sacrifice something for others. If we take back what was offered at the end of the Mass then the whole action was meaningless. Obvious gifts that might be offered include money, food for the poor, gifts at Christmas and Easter for less fortunate chil-

dren, etc. At a broader level a local parish might build con-
tacts with a Christian community elsewhere which is in great
need. This might be a community in the same country or in a
distant continent. Financial aid could be organised, profes-
sional help of various sorts could be offered and there could
be mutual exchanges of visitors. When representatives visit
from the other community they might be invited to speak at
Mass. All of this would contribute towards an enhanced sense
of common responsibility and sharing. What really matters in
the Mass is not the positioning of the candles or the flowers,
nor the quality of the music or the liturgical actions, but the
reality of commitment to one another and to the values of the
gospel that is fostered amongst the members of the community.
That is always a sobering thought.

4. Eucharistic Services

The emerging shortage of priests in many countries means
that communities must plan for services apart from Masses.
At such eucharistic services there is a penitential rite and a
liturgy of the word followed by the distribution of communion from the tabernacle and a dismissal. Thus it is that the
community assembles, the word is proclaimed and the body
of Christ is distributed but the absence of a priest means that
this is not a Mass since the eucharistic prayer is not said, the
Holy Spirit is not called upon the gifts and the sacrifice is not
offered. But such services are crucial to the life of any community which does not have a priest available either on a tem-
porary or more permanent basis. Nothing could be more
alien to the Catholic tradition than a failure to gather the people, even in the absence of a priest.

We shouldn't underestimate what these services might
achieve. The community would have to prepare for them by
selecting individuals to lead the services. Such people would
probably be older members of the community who have

given long witness to the values and practices of the church. Their role is to introduce the service and lead the penitential rite. Then a lector reads the scriptures, including the gospel; the lector or the leader might give a short reflection on the meaning of the scriptures for this community before the prayer of the faithful. The leader then invites all to recite the Lord's prayer and to offer one another the sign of peace, after which a eucharistic minister comes forward to distribute communion from the reserved sacrament in the tabernacle. The service concludes with the leader dismissing the community. The official texts request that the leader should not wear any liturgical dress nor sit in the presider's chair in order to avoid any confusion with the role of the priest.

Nobody should confuse such a service with a Mass, which is always the preferable option if a priest is available. But notice how closely one can tie such services to the Mass when one is aware of the four-fold nature of Christ's presence in the eucharist. It is also worth noting that such services clearly enhance the life of the local church; there is very mixed evidence from around the world as to whether the church is more alive where there is a shortage of priests or where they are plentiful. One way or the other, the community needs to gather in order to nourish and sustain its faith.

5. Relationship with the other sacraments

The eucharist is the source and summit of Christian life. The other six sacraments are related to and sustained by the eucharist. Take a look at the diagram. The eucharist gives us communion in the mystery of the death and resurrection of Christ. In baptism we receive new life in Christ, become members of the church and are freed from sin – the eucharist sustains and nourishes this new life. Through confirmation we are strengthened with the gift of God's Spirit to bear witness to our baptismal calling – in every eucharist we are also

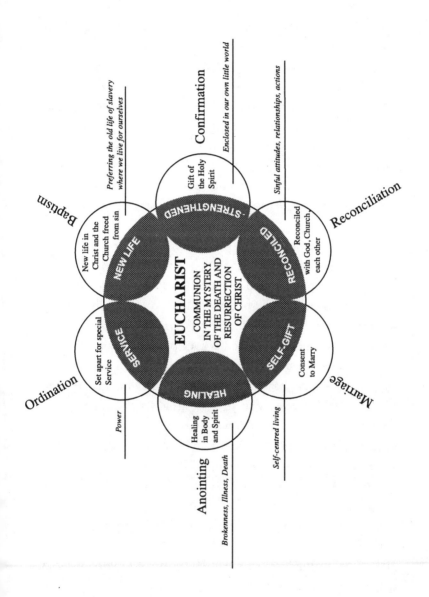

strengthened. In reconciliation we are reconciled to God, the community and one another – the eucharist always demands and creates reconciliation. Marriage demands that the couple give of themselves to each other – the eucharist is Christ's great self-gift which asks us to give of ourselves in return. In the sacrament of anointing, the sick, the old and the dying are healed in body and spirit – the eucharist endlessly seeks to bring healing into our lives. Those who are ordained are set apart for a special ministry of service to the community – the eucharist demands a life of service from all those who participate in it. The gift of new life and strength, the need for reconciliation and healing, the demand for self-giving and service form the foundation of the eucharist and the other six sacraments.

The sacraments concern real life. They challenge us to address attitudes and realities which are present in all of our lives. We can prefer the old life of slavery where we live only for ourselves enclosed in our own little world; our lives can be dominated by sinful attitudes, relationships or actions; the temptation to be self-centred is ever present; brokenness, illness and death touch all of us; we can abuse and manipulate the power that we have over others. The sacraments are a call to die to these realities so that we might rise to new life in Christ. The problem is that we might seldom, if ever, become aware of them and as a result the eucharist and the other sacraments can lose their meaning. Baptism loses its meaning for me if I'm happy with life as it is, confirmation loses its meaning for me if I think I can get along on my own, reconciliation loses its meaning for me if I have no sense of sin, marriage loses its meaning for me if I have no belief in self-giving, anointing loses its meaning for me if I'm not aware of the brokenness caused by illness and death, ordination loses its meaning for me if I only want to exercise power. Only when we face these issues honestly will we discover the demands and the liberation that the eucharistic mystery sets before us in terms of new life, strength, reconciliation, self-giving, healing and service. One way to do this is through rituals, reflections and role plays which awaken us to the presence of human limitations and sinfulness. These rituals and reflections can fulfil a very important function for they can prepare the way for the celebration of the sacraments, especially the eucharist. In some contexts it will be best not to celebrate the eucharist due to lack of faith or understanding or a proper disposition. In such situations we need to construct rituals and reflections which might awaken people to our crying need for redemption through new life and strength, reconciliation and healing, self-giving and service. The more aware we are of this need the better prepared we will be to celebrate the eucharist and the other sacraments. In the next chapter and in Appendix Two you will find suggestions for such rituals and reflections.

6. Anticipating the Final Banquet

Jesus' image for the end of time is the final nuptial banquet to which all are invited and where our hearts will be merry with the new wine of God's kingdom. In the meantime we get a foretaste of this banquet in the Mass. Since it is only a foretaste we eat only a morsel and drink only a sip but it is a morsel of the body of Christ and a sip of his blood. The transformation of the little bit of bread and the small portion of wine into the body and blood of Christ is a prophetic act anticipating now what will happen to all of reality in the future. Because we know our destiny we should be set free to act justly, to love tenderly and to walk humbly with our God (Micah 6:8). The Mass demands no less of us. Our eucharistic celebrations should be a counter-sign to the values of the world where might is always right and the powerful lord it over the weak. The bread is broken and the wine is poured out for a new world where poverty is overcome, oppression is rejected, hunger is satiated and thirst is quenched. In witnessing to the values of this new world, Christian communities need to act in a prophetic way. They can do this by making serious efforts to bring healing and hope into a broken world, by trying to alleviate grinding poverty, social exclusion and educational disadvantage in their own communities and throughout the world. The great temptation is to cling tenaciously to what we have; the invitation of the eucharist is to let go so that the new creation might begin to emerge.

God created the world; among the wonderful fruits of that creation are wheat and grapes; we create bread and wine from these gifts; God transforms our bread and wine into the body and blood of Christ; in God's new creation we too will be transformed. Our destiny is divine.

CHAPTER SIX

Being a Sacramental People

In this chapter we describe many different rituals. Some of the reflective texts used in these rituals can be found in Appendix Two. Our intention is that parishes or schools or retreat teams or other communities might adapt these texts and rituals to their own needs. We give a few suggestions as to their likely use but these are only broad guidelines. It is more important to use your imagination in adapting these ideas to your own context. Remember the basic premise of this book is that the key symbols of Christian initiation are more powerful than we ordinarily believe and that, if we allow them to speak, they could become a focus for renewal in the church. Just think of these symbols – water, oil, names, light, darkness, candles, bread, wine, the lamb, the bible, the table, the laying on of hands, the threshold. Interacting with these symbols breathes new life into our faith as without them it is little more than an intellectual claim but through them it becomes incarnate and communal. The only way to see if this works is to actually try it. You might be surprised by what you discover. Remember to keep in mind the principles we outlined in Chapter One.

1. Baptism

In the early church baptisms usually took place at Easter and the whole community participated in the preparation of the person who was going to be baptised. In fact this is the origin of Lent. Unfortunately today those that attend baptisms are often reduced to the role of spectators, taking no active role in the ritual. Here are some simple ideas to encourage greater participation in the rite of baptism for a child.

Naming

In the rite the priest asks what name is to be given to the child. The naming of a person is an important Christian tradition. When the disciples were called to follow Jesus some were given different names. Simon was called Peter while James and John the sons of Zebedee were called 'Sons of Thunder' by Jesus (Mk 3:13-19). Zechariah, John the Baptist's father, was struck dumb by a visitation of an angel but received his gift of speech back when he uttered the name of his new child, 'John' (Lk 1:59-66). The naming of infants at baptism marks their incorporation into Christ and the Christian community. A parent or grandparent or friend could give the story behind the name that is chosen. There is a story behind every name. For example, if the name is taken from a deceased relative or a saint, a story could be told about that person and perhaps as to how he/she witnessed to the faith during his/her life.

The Word

After the readings, the following Rite of the Word could be used. This should all take place at the ambo.

The proclamation of the word is central to baptism. From the earliest moments of the church those who were baptised responded to the word of God. The scriptures play a key role in the celebrations and rituals of the community. We learn the story of our faith from them and we learn our history and our identity. Unfortunately today there are many Christian homes which do not have a bible. Considering the amount of money that can now be spent on celebrations after the baptism, perhaps it would be a good idea to present a bible to the parents of the baptised infant. It could be a present from the Godparents. There is a strong tradition that when Jesus was born he was given gifts. Certainly this is something that could be done at the baptism of a couple's first child, or perhaps every child should be given their own copy of the scriptures on the day of their baptism. The following rite or something like it could accompany such a presentation.

Godparents to the parents: On behalf of (name) receive this gift of the sacred scriptures. We hope that you will share the stories of our faith with (name) and teach him/her the power and the wisdom that is contained in the word of God.

The book is then handed over.

Parents: On behalf of (name) we thank you for this gift. We will place this sacred text in a place of prominence in our house and we will do our best to share with (name) the stories, parables and prayers of these sacred scriptures.

Water

After the priest pours the water over the infant the following text could be used to involve all present in this important symbol of baptism.

Reader: In the Old Testament the Hebrews were slaves in Egypt but God brought them out of slavery to freedom through the waters of the Red Sea. Water is a symbol for the new life that Christians have in Christ: a life free from the slavery of sin, a life full of the promise of Easter.

Priest: I invite you all to come forward and bless yourselves with the waters of baptism.

As people go to the water they bless themselves after dipping their hands into the baptismal font.

All: We revisit the waters of our baptism, the waters of Easter and new life,
in the name of the Father
and of the Son
and of the Holy Spirit.
Amen.

All present should be encouraged to bring some of the holy water from the baptismal font with them to be used at home.

Chrism

The anointing with chrism is one of the most important aspects of the baptismal ceremony but the one that modern people find most difficult to appreciate. This problem is heightened by our minimalist use of oil in the sacrament. In order to encourage a greater understanding of the significance of oil in Christian tradition some of the following ideas could be used.

(a) A large container of chrism could be kept beside the baptismal font throughout the year and in this way people would become more aware of its role within the rites of the church. This container could be decorated and highlighted in various ways. During every baptism some oil would be taken from this container for use in the particular ceremony.

(b) The story of oil needs to be retold. Local children could be invited to prepare a visual presentation depicting the story of oil. This could be done through drama, painting, poetry, writing, etc. A great source of ideas for this can be found in the prayer of blessing of chrism in the Holy Thursday Chrism Mass. The prayer that the bishop says is:

God our Maker,
source of all growth in holiness,
accept the joyful thanks and praise
we offer in the name of your church.

In the beginning, at your command,
the earth produced fruit-bearing trees.
From the fruit of the olive tree
you have provided us with oil for holy chrism.
The prophet David sang of the life and joy
that the oil would bring us in the sacraments of your love.

After the avenging flood,
the dove returning to Noah with an olive branch
announced your gift of peace.
This was a sign of a greater gift to come.
Now the waters of baptism wash away the sins of humanity,
and by the anointing with olive oil
you make us radiant with your joy.

At your command,
Aaron was washed with water,
and your servant Moses, his brother,
anointed him priest.
This too foreshadowed greater things to come.
After your son, Jesus Christ our Lord,
asked John for baptism in the waters of Jordan,
you sent the Spirit upon him
in the form of a dove
and by the witness of your own voice
you declared him to be your only, well-beloved Son.
In this you clearly fulfilled the prophecy of David,
that Christ would be anointed with the oil of gladness
beyond his fellow men.

And so, Father, we ask you to bless this oil you have created.
Fill it with the power of your Holy Spirit
through Christ your Son.
It is from him that chrism takes its name
and with chrism you have anointed
for yourself priests and kings,
prophets and martyrs.

Make this chrism a sign of life and salvation
for those who are to be born again in the waters of baptism.
Wash away the evil they have inherited from sinful Adam,
and when they are anointed with this holy oil
make them temples of your glory,
radiant with the goodness of new life
that has its source in you.

Through this sign of chrism
grant them royal, priestly, and prophetic honour,
and clothe them with incorruption.
Let this be indeed the chrism of salvation
for those who will be born again of water and the Holy Spirit.
May they come to share eternal life
in the glory of your kingdom.

This text could be used as a basis for the writing of the story of the significance of oil in Christianity.

(c) The following text is particularly suitable for use during the chrismation because the child is being anointed with God's Holy Spirit.

Two readers are needed, one reads the spirit of the world and the other the spirit of God. In each case the spirit of the world comes first, followed within a couple of seconds by the spirit of God; there is then a substantial pause (10-15 seconds) before moving on. Ideally the two readers should stand at lecterns at opposite ends of the relevant space.

1   The spirit of the world says that externals are all important – looks, property, possessions. You are what you have.

2   The spirit of God says that your looks and appearance can be very deceptive. You must look into the heart, into the depth of life to see who we really are.

1   The spirit of the world says that life is a test and success is everything. It abhors failure and disappointment.

2   The spirit of God says that failure can be more important than success. We can learn much even from the sad and more difficult times.

1   The spirit of the world says that the great problems – unemployment, ecology, violence – have nothing to do with me. I've just got to mind my own patch.

2   The spirit of God says that I am responsible for everyone, everywhere, at all times. There are no strangers in God's eyes.

1   The spirit of the world says that love is about things going well, in accord with my plans.

2   The spirit of God says that love is about giving of myself, even when I feel that I cannot.

1   The spirit of the world says that there is no such thing as forgiveness because there is no such thing as sin.

2   The spirit of God says that forgiveness is the greatest reality that we know. We sin, we fail, yet we can be freed to go on.

1   The spirit of the world says that honesty and commitment are impossible and don't really exist.

2   The spirit of God says that honesty and commitment are the only things that really matter in the end.

1   The spirit of the world says that the sick and the disabled are not really alive. Sickness and disability are disastrous.

2   The spirit of God says that the sick and the disabled are often those who are most alive for they know their dependence; they know that life is not in their control.

1   The spirit of the world says that death is the end of life and proves that life is futile.

2 The spirit of God says that death is not the end of life as the great spirit present in us is not extinguished but transformed.

The Paschal Candle

During baptism a special candle that is kept by the family is lit from the paschal candle. The paschal candle reminds us of the centrality of Easter for we are baptised into the death and resurrection of Jesus; we are baptised into Easter. There is no reason why everyone present cannot have his or her own candle that can be lit from the paschal candle and then brought home. Often today our Christian homes are devoid of any sacred symbols. But since there is now a greater interest in the use of candles, we should surely adapt this trend to foster a renewed sense of Christian symbolism. This rite or something like it could be used after the parents have lit their own candle.

Each person should be given his or her own lighted candle.

Reader: After Christ's death his disciples were frightened and dejected in the upper room. Then the Spirit of God came upon them in tongues of fire and transformed them to become men and women of courage and faith. The paschal candle reminds us that we are baptised into Christ's death and resurrection. We are a people who must often endure darkness and despair, yet the light of Christ reminds us that we are an Easter people who live with the promise of new life and happiness.

Priest: We ask God to bless these candles and make them sacred. Receive the light of Christ. Receive the light of hope and new life.

All: We are an Easter people baptised in the death and resurrection of Jesus Christ. We will bring this light of Easter into our home, making it a sacred place.

2. Eucharist

The most significant ritual and occasion of gathering together for Catholics is to celebrate the eucharist. Yet if there is one failing which plagues all ritual celebrations it is a lack of knowledge or understanding of what is going on. This, of course, does not make the sacrament invalid but it does take away from the profound fruit that it might bear in a person's life. Many priests, parents, liturgists, catechists and parish groups strive courageously each year to make the Mass more interesting, trying their best to get more young people to participate. All these efforts should be commended and no doubt many are worthwhile and enriching.

Here we try to provide some rituals, which could be used during any of the Sundays throughout the year, but more appropriately on the three Sundays of Lent before Palm Sunday. The aims are catechetical insofar as these rites attempt to focus the attention of the assembly onto the meaning behind the eucharist.

First Sunday

If these rites were used during Lent, then week 1 would occur on the third Sunday of Lent. An ideal time for these rites would be after the reading of the gospel.

This rite aims to tell the story of the Passover, to highlight the sacrifice of the unblemished lamb and celebrate the people's redemption and freedom from slavery. In order to make this rite physically striking, a threshold should be built in the sanctuary. It can be decorated lavishly because it will remain the centrepiece for the remaining Sundays. It is important that the lintel is easily recognisable. It should be noted that these rites would demand preparation and the involvement of many in the community. The threshold should remain standing in the sanctuary for the duration of these special weeks.

Local schools could be asked to provide posters depicting the events of the Exodus. The story of this great moment of liberation could be written up around the church along with the visual depictions. Over these weeks the church and sanctuary could be transformed into a place celebrating this great ritual and story.

Rite of Passover

Reader: Many years before Christ, our forebears, the Hebrews, were slaves in Egypt. The people of God cried out for deliverance from the burden of slavery. God heard their cries and on the night of the Passover they were instructed to take an unblemished lamb, sacrifice it and place its blood on the lintel of their door posts. That night the angel of the Lord passed over the houses of the Hebrew slaves but brought death to their Egyptian taskmasters.

At this point a person takes a brush with red paint and brushes the paint all over the lintel of the threshold.

Reader: The next day the Hebrews were ordered out of Egypt and they passed through the waters of the Red Sea into the freedom of the Promised Land.

Attention should then turn to the baptismal font. A person or couple should pour a large amount of water into the baptismal font.

Reader: It was through water that our forebears, the people of God, gained their freedom and redemption. Through the waters of baptism we are set free from sin and fear, and pass, as if through a doorway, into the very life of God.

Attention should then turn to the altar as a person or couple brings the bread and wine to the altar for the eucharist.

Reader: It was through the blood of the lamb that our forebears, the people of God, gained their freedom and their redemption. Today we celebrate the redemption that Christ won for us by receiving his body and blood, since he is truly the new Lamb of God.

Second Sunday

In order to make this Sunday different, batches of unleavened bread should be used. This requires planning and preparation but it is worthwhile because it demands an effort from the community. People could be asked to bake the bread beforehand and bring it to Mass. Enough bread should be prepared for the congregation. At the threshold, however, a pan should be prepared over some heat so that some bread can actually be baked during this rite.

Rite of Unleavened Bread

Reader: At the time of the Passover the people of God had to hurry from the land of Egypt. They had to prepare to leave in haste and so they were told that for seven days they were only to eat unleavened bread, for they had no time to wait for the yeast to rise in leavened bread. And so the people baked unleavened bread.

At this point some unleavened dough should be put on the pan at the threshold. This bread will not be used for the eucharist.

Reader: We bake unleavened bread because we are waiting for the promise of our God to deliver us from the death of slavery.

The previously prepared unleavened bread should then be brought up to the priest at the altar.

Priest: Every time the Jews celebrated their freedom through the Passover, they cooked unleavened bread for the Passover meal. On the night that Jesus celebrated the Last Supper, he took the unleavened bread and broke it to share it amongst his disciples.

As the bread will be broken during the eucharist, the following text could be used now or at the Lamb of God. This could be done using many readers placed around the church or sanctuary.

Reader: Our ancestors were a broken people.

• When we broke our relationship with God through sin we were expelled from the paradise that was Eden.

• In Egypt our hearts were broken by the burden and torture of slavery.

• In the Old Testament the prophets told us that we were not obeying the will of God. Constantly we broke our relationship with the God who had freed us from slavery.

At this point some local school children could bring posters to the altar and put them up depicting the turmoil and sinfulness of today's world. Again different readers can be used.

Reader: Today we are a broken people.

• Many people throughout the world are broken through famine, torture and injustice.

• Many in our own community are suffering from loss, loneliness and isolation. They yearn for a better future.

• Through neglect and selfishness we all bear the responsibility for the pain and suffering of our brothers and sisters throughout the world.

The advantage of using this text at the Lamb of God, when the bread is actually broken, is that it brings together the themes of the two Sundays, i.e. the passover lamb and the unleavened bread. Alternatively, a text like the following might be used during the recitation of the Lamb of God.

All say: Lamb of God who takes away the sins of the world, have mercy on us.

Reader: Christ went to the cross as an innocent lamb. He offered himself as a sacrifice so that our sins might be taken away.

All say: Lamb of God who takes away the sins of the world, have mercy on us.

Reader: As the priest breaks the bread he is breaking Christ's body which was broken for us on the cross.

All say: Lamb of God who takes away the sins of the world, grant us peace.

Reader: As we eat the Body of Christ we already share that peace which will be complete at the end of time. We are not yet fully at peace, but in this communion with one another and with God we already overcome all brokeness and division.

Post-communion reflection (the following text could be used):

> *Take, bless, break and give.*
> In the Eucharist bread is taken, blessed, broken and given.
> In life we are taken, blessed, broken and given.
> The priest takes the bread in his hands and blesses it during the eucharistic prayer;
> then he breaks it and it is given to us as the body of Christ.
> Through our birth and baptism we are taken into God's hands;
> as the bread is taken, so too are we.
> In life we are blessed by family, friends, love and joy;
> as the bread is blessed, so too are we.
> We are broken by failure, sin, pain and heartbreak;
> as the bread is broken, so too are we.
> In death we are given back to the mystery from which we came;
> as the bread is given, so too are we.
> When we take, bless, break and give bread to one another,
> we believe the Lord to be especially present in our midst.
> But we must learn to accept that in his memory
> we will be taken, blessed, broken and given
> for the life of the world.

Third Sunday

The emphasis in week three is on the eucharist as thanksgiving. In this celebration all the members of the congregation will receive communion under both species.

Reader: In the Old Testament the people of God offered the first fruits of the harvest in thanksgiving for the blessings that Yahweh had bestowed upon them. The Jewish people celebrated their freedom from Egypt in the Passover meal with bread and wine.

At this point jugs of wine should be brought to the altar from around the church.

Reader: We offer this wine to God in thanksgiving for the gift of his Son Jesus who offered himself as a sacrifice for the sins of the whole of humankind. Through the pouring of his blood on Calvary we have been reconciled to our Father.

At this point baskets of food should be brought up to the threshold and placed around it.

Reader: In the Passover the Jews celebrate their passing through the waters of the Red Sea. They reached the land of God's promise, a land rich with milk and honey. The people lived off the land and experienced the generosity of God. We offer these baskets of food and aid to the poor of this community so that all amongst us can experience the blessings and bounty of a new life in Christ.

3. The renewal of baptism

People gather in a dark space, preferably at night-time. The ritual revolves around darkness, water, oil and the renewal of baptismal promises. Two voices are required: the leader and a questioner (preferably the youngest person present).

As the people gather there should be gentle music and dimmed lighting. As the music fades all lights should be extinguished.

Questioner: Why are we sitting here in the dark?

Leader: When God created the world there was darkness over the deep and God's Spirit hovered over the chaos. God said, 'Let there be light' and there was light. God saw that the light was good. *(Pause)*

In the heart of every person lurks darkness and light, the darkness of self-doubt and despair and the light of hope and self-worth. *(Pause)*

The prophets of old foretold a time when the people who walked in darkness would see a great light and for those who lived in a land of deep shadow a light would shine. *(Pause)*

The early Christians spoke of Jesus as the light that had come into the world and so they gathered in the evening darkness to commemorate his life. And then they lit a candle to celebrate his presence amongst them.

The Paschal candle is lit, followed by a pause and then there is a song or reflective music with the theme of 'light'. During this, each individual's candle should be lit.

With the room bathed in candlelight our attention now turns to the oil. Ideally the fragrance of oil should scent the room.

Questioner: Why is there such a strong smell of oil?

Leader: One of the great gifts of God's creation is fruit-bearing trees. From the fruit of the olive tree oil is pressed. In
the Old Testament people were anointed with oil to make
them sacred. Of old, the Jews spoke of David as God's
anointed, the one set apart to be their king. The early
Christians spoke of Jesus as the new David and so they
called him Christ which means 'the anointed one'. In baptism we were anointed with the oil of chrism through
which the Spirit of Christ was given to us. This Spirit
makes us temples of God's glory bearing the very fragrance
of Christ himself.

*Everyone is smeared with oil on the forehead while the leader says
to each individual:*

You were anointed in baptism like Christ as priest, prophet
and king. God's favour rests on you.

*As people are being anointed with oil there is music or song. Then
our attention turns to the water.*

Questioner: Why are there big jugs of water over there?

*Two people pour water slowly from the jugs into a large container.
During this the leader says:*

At the very dawn of creation, God's Spirit breathed on the
waters.

The waters of the great flood brought an end to sin and a
new beginning of goodness.

Through the waters of the Red Sea, God led Israel out of
slavery.

In the waters of the Jordan, Jesus was baptised by John and
anointed with the Spirit.

When Jesus hung on the cross, blood and water flowed
from his side.

In baptism, we were baptised with water in the name of
the Father and of the Son and of the Holy Spirit.

The leader sprinkles everyone with water saying:
> You were baptised in the name of the Father and of the Son and of the Holy Spirit.

Alternatively, people come forward and bless themselves with the water saying:
> I believe in God the Father and the Son and the Holy Spirit.

As people are being sprinkled with water there is music or song.
The last aspect of the ritual is renewal of baptismal promises.

Leader: Do you believe in God the creator of light and darkness, land and sea, heaven and earth, woman and man?

All: We do.

Leader: Do you cherish and protect the earth as God's creation?

All: We do.

Leader: Do you appreciate the gift of water which endlessly renews and sustains life?

All: We do.

Leader: Do you give thanks for the spring and the summer, the sowing and the harvest, the sun and the moon, the wind and the rain, the mountain top and the sea shore?

All: We do.

Leader: Do you believe that in the midst of a beautiful world we, like Adam and Eve, live in the shadow of temptation and evil?

All: We do.

Leader: Do you reject all that is evil?

All: We do.

Leader: Do you reject injustice, hatred, despair and bigotry?

All: We do.

Leader: Do you reject all that undermines and destroys the gift of life?

All: We do.

Leader: Do you believe that Jesus Christ is the Saviour of the world?

All: We do.

Leader: Do you believe that Jesus died for us on Calvary and was raised from the dead?

All: We do.

Leader: Do you believe that in baptism you became followers of Jesus?

All: We do.

Leader: Do you believe that when you were anointed with oil in baptism you received the gift of God's Spirit?

All: We do.

Leader: Do you believe that God's Spirit is present in humanity and that our destiny is to share fully in God's own life?

All: We do.

Leader: Do you accept the Christian identity that was given to you in your name at baptism?

All: We do.

Leader: Do you accept that your faith can only be lived with others in a Christian community?

All: We do.

Leader: Do you believe that the church, a community of saints and sinners, is the temple of God's presence in the world?

All: We do.

Leader: Do you take responsibility for the future well-being of the church?

All: We do.

Leader: Do you believe in the final triumph of Christ over sin, light over darkness, truth over lies, hope over despair, good over evil and life over death?

All: We do.

Leader: Do you today, in the presence of fellow believers, confirm the meaning and implications of your baptism?

All: We do.

Leader: Do you now promise to live your life in accordance with the Christian faith which we have professed together?

All: We do.

Leader: Then may God bless you and strengthen you as you bear witness to your faith.

The ritual concludes with the singing of a baptismal song.

4. A celebration with parents
before the confirmation of their children.

In order to emphasise the baptismal roots of confirmation, the previous ritual on the renewal of baptism should be used. This could be enhanced by weaving other relevant texts into the ceremony. The rite concludes with the parents renewing their own baptismal promises in anticipation of what their children will do in the near future.

People gather in a dark space, preferably at night-time. The ritual revolves around darkness, water, oil and the renewal of baptismal promises. Two voices are required: the leader and a questioner.

As the people gather there should be gentle music and dimmed lighting. As the music fades all lights should be extinguished.

Questioner: Why are we sitting here in the dark?

Leader: When God created the world there was darkness over the deep and God's Spirit hovered over the chaos. God said, 'Let there be light' and there was light. God saw that the light was good. *(Pause)*

In the heart of every person lurks darkness and light, the darkness of self-doubt and despair and the light of hope and self-worth. *(Pause)*

The prophets of old foretold a time when the people who walked in darkness would see a great light and for those who lived in a land of deep shadow a light would shine. *(Pause)*

The early Christians spoke of Jesus as the light that had come into the world and so they gathered in the evening darkness to commemorate his life. And then they lit a candle to celebrate his presence amongst them.

The Paschal candle is lit, followed by a pause and then there is a
song or reflective music with the theme of 'light'. During this each
individual's candle should be lit. Then one of the parents reads
the following text:

> *Letting go*
> Lord God help me to let go.
> Life is an endless process of letting go;
> In our birth we had to let go of the security of our mother's
> womb and emerge into a strange world;
> In adolescence we let go of the innocence of childhood;
> All of us have to let go of home, parents must let go of
> their children and children must let go of their parents;
> Throughout life as we grow and mature we must continu-
> ally let go of opinions, jobs, good health and ultimately of
> the idea that we are in control.
> And, of course, in death we must let go of those we love.
> Between womb and tomb life is an endless process of letting go.
> Come, Holy Spirit, help me to let go so that even when the
> letting go is tearful and sad it will awaken me to the mystery
> and wonder of life.
> Life is the greatest gift we have received and we must in the
> end let go of this gift.
> We must let go of the past to let God be the God of the
> future.

With the room bathed in candlelight our attention now turns to
the oil. Ideally the fragrance of oil should scent the room.

Questioner: Why is there such a strong smell of oil?

Leader: One of the great gifts of God's creation is fruit-bearing trees. From the fruit of the olive tree oil is pressed. In
the Old Testament people were anointed with oil to make
them sacred. Of old the Jews spoke of David as God's
anointed, the one set apart to be their king. The early
Christians spoke of Jesus as the new David and so they

called him Christ which means 'the anointed one'. In baptism and confirmation we were anointed with the oil of chrism through which the Spirit of Christ was given to us. This Spirit makes us temples of God's glory bearing the very fragrance of Christ himself.

Everyone is smeared with oil on the forehead while the leader says to each individual,

You were anointed in baptism and confirmation like Christ as priest, prophet and king. God's favour rests on you.

As people are being anointed with oil there is music or song. Then two parents read the following text, one reads the spirit of the world and the other the spirit of God. In each case the spirit of the world comes first followed within a couple of seconds by the spirit of God; there is then a substantial pause (10-15 seconds) before moving on. Ideally the two readers should stand at lecterns at opposite ends of the relevant space.

The leader introduces the text as follows:

All of us have been baptised and confirmed with God's Spirit. But we are always tempted to live in accord with the values of the spirit of the world. As your children prepare to be anointed again with God's Spirit, we need to reflect on the reality that faces them in the future.

1 The spirit of the world says that externals are all important – looks, property, possessions. You are what you have.
2 The spirit of God says that your looks and appearance can be very deceptive. You must look into the heart, into the depth of life to see who we really are.
1 The spirit of the world says that life is a test and success is everything. It abhors failure and disappointment.
2 The spirit of God says that failure can be more important than success. We can learn much even from the sad and more difficult times.

1 The spirit of the world says that the great problems – unemployment, ecology, violence – have nothing to do with me. I've just got to mind my own patch.

2 The spirit of God says that I am responsible for everyone, everywhere, at all times. There are no strangers in God's eyes.

1 The spirit of the world says that love is about things going well, in accord with my plans.

2 The spirit of God says that love is about giving of myself, even when I feel that I cannot.

1 The spirit of the world says that there is no such thing as forgiveness because there is no such thing as sin.

2 The spirit of God says that forgiveness is the greatest reality that we know. We sin, we fail, yet we can be freed to go on.

1 The spirit of the world says that honesty and commitment are impossible and don't really exist.

2 The spirit of God says that honesty and commitment are the only things that really matter in the end.

1 The spirit of the world says that the sick and the disabled are not really alive. Sickness and disability are disastrous.

2 The spirit of God says that the sick and the disabled are often those who are most alive for they know their dependence; they know that life is not in their control.

1 The spirit of the world says that death is the end of life and proves that life is futile.

2 The spirit of God says that death is not the end of life as the great spirit present in us is not extinguished but transformed.

Then our attention turns to the water.

Questioner: Why are there big jugs of water over there?

Two people pour water slowly from the jugs into a large container. During this the leader says:

At the very dawn of creation God's Spirit breathed on the waters.

The waters of the great flood brought an end to sin and a new beginning of goodness.

Through the waters of the Red Sea God led Israel out of slavery.

In the waters of the Jordan Jesus was baptised by John and anointed with the spirit.

When Jesus hung on the cross blood and water flowed from his side.

In baptism we were baptised with water in the name of the Father and of the Son and of the Holy Spirit.

The leader sprinkles everyone with water saying:

You were baptised in the name of the Father and of the Son and of the Holy Spirit.

Alternatively people come forward and bless themselves with the water saying:

I believe in God the Father and the Son and the Holy Spirit.

As people are being sprinkled with water there is music or song. Then the following text is read by one or more readers.

The community of Pentecost

Remember the famous scene in the upper room when the disciples and Mary were waiting for the gift of the Spirit. Did you ever think much about the reality that they faced? In many ways that group, which included Mary the Mother of Jesus, was very akin to our gathering here today. Some people in the upper room were doubtful about what it was all about; similarly some of us here are doubtful, wondering if we should be here at all.

Some were enthusiastic, bursting to tell the message to others; undoubtedly some of us are enthusiastic to get out there and tell people the good news.

Some of the disciples were very confused by everything that had happened to them; some of us are very confused by what has happened to us in our lives.

Some of the folk had grown cynical about the whole thing, believing that they had been fooled; maybe some of us have grown cynical too, having seen so much that disheartens us in the church and in religion in general.

Some of the disciples were broken by all the suffering and death they had witnessed; some of us are broken by life, by illness, by death.

Others of the disciples were worried and didn't know where to turn; some of us carry great worries about what the future holds.

Presumably some of the people in the upper room were bored, wondering if anything was ever going to happen; some of us probably find life tedious and wonder if it has any value. And finally there were those who were deeply hopeful in the midst of it all, trusting in God's promise; equally there are people of deep hope and joy sitting in our midst today. So if you count yourself somewhere, anywhere, amongst those who are doubtful, enthusiastic, confused, cynical, broken, worried, bored, hopeful or joyful, then take great heart for it was to such as these that the Spirit of God was first given. It was to a motley crew like ourselves that God gave the greatest gift: not to those who had all the answers, nor to those who had life all sewn up, but rather to those who were struggling with the realities of life. On (date) our children will be confirmed with the gift of God's Spirit. They have already received the great gift of life in childbirth and they were anointed with God's Spirit in baptism. Now the bishop will confirm them in their Christian calling with the gift of the seven-fold Spirit. If we are truly to accompany our children on their journey to Christian maturity we need to renew our own baptismal promises.

The last aspect of the ritual is the renewal of baptismal promises.

Leader: Do you believe in God the creator of light and darkness, land and sea, heaven and earth, woman and man?
All: We do.
Leader: Do you cherish and protect the earth as God's creation?
All: We do.
Leader: Do you appreciate the gift of water which endlessly renews and sustains life?
All: We do.
Leader: Do you give thanks for the spring and the summer, the sowing and the harvest, the sun and the moon, the wind and the rain, the mountain top and the sea shore?
All: We do.
Leader: Do you believe that in the midst of a beautiful world we, like Adam and Eve, live in the shadow of temptation and evil?
All: We do.
Leader: Do you reject all that is evil?
All: We do.
Leader: Do you reject injustice, hatred, despair and bigotry?
All: We do.
Leader: Do you reject all that undermines and destroys the gift of life?
All: We do.
Leader: Do you believe that Jesus Christ is the Saviour of the world?
All: We do.
Leader: Do you believe that Jesus died for us on Calvary and was raised from the dead?
All: We do.
Leader: Do you believe that in baptism you became followers of Jesus?
All: We do.

Leader: Do you believe that when you were anointed with oil in baptism you received the gift of God's Spirit?

All: We do.

Leader: Do you believe that God's Spirit is present in humanity and that our destiny is to share fully in God's own life?

All: We do.

Leader: Do you accept the Christian identity that was given to you in your name at baptism?

All: We do.

Leader: Do you accept that your faith can only be lived with others in a Christian community?

All: We do.

Leader: Do you believe that the church, a community of saints and sinners, is the temple of God's presence in the world?

All: We do.

Leader: Do you take responsibility for the future well-being of the church?

All: We do.

Leader: Do you believe in the final triumph of Christ over sin, light over darkness, truth over lies, hope over despair, good over evil and life over death?

All: We do.

Leader: Do you today, in the presence of fellow believers, confirm the meaning and implications of your baptism?

All: We do.

Leader: Do you promise to accompany your child who will soon be confirmed on the journey to Christian maturity?

All: We do.

Leader: Do you now promise to live your life in accordance with the Christian faith which we have professed together?

All: We do.

Leader: Then may God bless you and strengthen you as you bear witness to your faith.

The ritual concludes with the singing of a song related to the Holy Spirit.

The children who are to be confirmed could prepare the space for this ritual beforehand. They could make posters and paintings relating to the various aspects of the celebration. They could prepare a parchment for each parent and sponsor which would include the baptismal promises above and the name of the places in which the parent/sponsor was baptised and confirmed along with the names of their parents and Godparents. As part of this ritual, parents/sponsors might be asked to sign this parchment.

5. A missioning ceremony
after a significant shared experience.

The shared experience might be a retreat, a pilgrimage, an assembly or meeting over several days or weeks. In anticipation of this final gathering, each participant should be asked to bring along some object which symbolises something of the meaning of the experience for him/her. There are three parts to the ritual, namely word, faith and community. If this celebration is incorporated in a Mass, the first part (word) will form part of the liturgy of the word; the second element (faith) will take the place of the homily, creed and prayers of the faithful; whilst the third section (community) will occur after communion and include the final blessing. It is crucial that all participants are sitting in a circle.

(a) Word

The intention of this part of the ritual is to intertwine the story of each individual present with that of the scriptures. The following text is read.

In each case a personal reflection comes first, followed after a pause by a biblical quotation; there is then a further pause before moving on. Ideally the two readers should stand at lecterns at opposite ends of the relevant space.

1   We are children of the earth, made of the same stuff as the stars, we are part of the beauty of the earth.
2   In the beginning God created the heavens and the earth. Now the earth was a formless void, there was darkness over the deep and God's Spirit hovered over the water. God saw what God had made and it was very good.
1   Think of the date you were born, the joy of your parents, family, neighbours and friends. Imagine yourself as a baby.
2   Before I formed you in the womb I knew you, before you came to birth I consecrated you.

1 Recall in your own mind the various places you've lived.
   Think of the houses, the places – go into each of them in
   your mind.
2 Wherever you go, I will go, wherever you live I will live.
1 Think of a couple of really happy moments in your life.
   Treasure them in your heart.
2 I want you to be happy, always happy in the Lord; I repeat,
   what I want is your happiness.
1 Allow moments of suffering and pain to enter your mind.
   They are part of who we are.
2 Come to me all you who labour and are overburdened and
   I will give you rest. For my yoke is easy and my burden is
   light.
1 Who are the people who accompany you? – family, spouse,
   children, neighbours, friends? Look at their faces now.
2 Did not our hearts burn within us as he talked to us on the
   road and explained the scriptures to us ... and their eyes
   were opened and they recognised him in the breaking of
   the bread.
1 What do you hope for? What are your greatest expecta-
   tions, your cherished dream?
2 What we suffer in this life can never be compared to the
   glory which is yet to be revealed.
1 Where will it all end? What will happen in the future?
2 I saw a new heaven and a new earth ... Then I heard a
   loud voice call from above: now I am making the whole of
   creation new.

*After this the leader should take a large bible or lectionary and
hold it wide open over the head of each participant and say:*

God's word has been sown in your heart; you are God's
word to the world.

(b) Faith

A text reflecting on the nature of life as journey is read; this could be Luke's account of the disciples on the road to Emmaus. (An alternative text is Acts of the Apostles 11:1-10.) After this the leader asks all present to present their symbols. As individuals speak of the meaning or story behind their symbols, they will inevitably tell something of what has happened to them during their time together. The symbols should be laid down together in the middle of the group (if the text from Acts has been used the symbols should be put on a sheet opened on the ground). As much time as needs be must be devoted to this part of the ritual. At the end, the leader blesses the symbols with water while the group sings a song with the theme of 'journey', or there is instrumental music.

(c) Community

To finish, all the participants are asked to take their personal symbols and stand in a circle facing inwards. As they face inwards towards each other, the text of 1 Corinthians 12:4-27 is read. They are then told to turn around and face away from the circle. The priest, or if there is no priest the elder of the gathering, blesses all present in these or similar words:

> You are the salt of the earth,
> you are the light of the world,
> together we are the body of Christ.
> As a baby you were baptised in Christ,
> at seven years you were invited to eat from the altar of God,
> and later the church confirmed the gift of God's Spirit given
> to you.
> Go now from this holy place,
> treasure in your heart the wonder of who you are
> and may the words you have heard here ever echo in your
> mind.

You are the salt of the earth,
   you are the light of the world,
      together we are the body of Christ.

This ritual should come at the very end of the gathering. Once it is finished people should disperse.

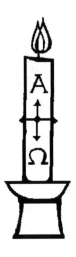

6. Celebrating death and new life

It is part of the rhythm of the natural world that something must die before new life can begin. We need support and encouragement to integrate this reality into our own lives. This ritual attempts to awaken us to the ache of loss and the need to let go.

Participants should gather in a dark room with a little candlelight. Symbols of death should abound. Bones or candles should be placed at four points to create a rectangle shape on the ground. Then the following text is read:

Letting go
Lord God help me to let go.
Life is an endless process of letting go;
In our birth we had to let go of the security of our mother's womb and emerge into a strange world;
In adolescence we let go of the innocence of childhood;
All of us have to let go of home, parents must let go of their children and children must let go of their parents;
Throughout life as we grow and mature we must continually let go of opinions, jobs, good health and ultimately of the idea that we are in control.
And, of course, in death we must let go of those we love.
Between womb and tomb life is an endless process of letting go.
Come, Holy Spirit, help me to let go so that even when the letting go is tearful and sad it will awaken me to the mystery and wonder of life.
Life is the greatest gift we have received and we must in the end let go of this gift.
We must let go of the past to let God be the God of the future.

After the reading an older person could speak from a very real and human perspective of the need to let go in life.

Then one by one each individual lies down on the ground within the shape of the grave made by the candles and bones. As each person is lying on the ground another member of the group reads as follows (some soft singing or humming in the background can be very evocative):

> You are not afraid of dying to the old,
> You are not afraid of giving birth to what is new,
> You are not afraid of planting,
> You are not afraid of uprooting what has been planted,
> You are not afraid of searching,
> You are not afraid of keeping or throwing away,
> You are not afraid of tears or mourning,
> You are not afraid of laughter.

The ritual finishes with the reading of Ecclesiastes 3:1-8:

> For everything there is a season, and a time for every matter under heaven:
> a time to be born, and a time to die;
> a time to plant, and a time to pluck up what is planted;
> a time to kill, and a time to heal;
> a time to break down, and a time to build up;
> a time to weep, and a time to laugh;
> a time to mourn, and a time to dance;
> a time to throw away stones, and a time to gather stones together;
> a time to embrace, and a time to refrain from embracing;
> a time to seek, and a time to lose;
> a time to keep, and a time to throw away;
> a time to tear, and a time to sew;
> a time to keep silence, and a time to speak;
> a time to love, and a time to hate;
> a time for war, and a time for peace.

7. Rites of Affirmation

The rite of affirmation is intended to highlight the gifts of various adults within the community – women, men, priests. Each group is called forward separately. They go to the front of the assembly where they stand facing the leader/elders whilst the others remain seated. Then the following texts are read aloud by the leader/elders. Immediately afterwards they place an open bible over the head of each individual and say: 'God's word has been sown in your heart. You are God's word.'

Rite of Affirmation for Women

All women present are called forward and stand at the front of the assembly.

Ruth (first voice): Ruth's mother-in-law was called Naomi and she had lost both her sons. In desperation and loneliness she decided to return to her homeland. She told Ruth that she had no more sons and that life with her had no future. However Ruth did not desert her mother-in-law. She said to her: 'Wherever you go I will go, wherever you live I will live.'

Pause

May you like Ruth be blessed with faithfulness and perseverance. As pilgrims on the journey of life, may you remain steadfast in your faith even in the midst of disillusionment and disappointment.

Mary of Magdala (second voice): After the resurrection, and whilst the followers of Jesus cowered in despair and fear, Mary of Magdala set out to tend the body of Jesus. Through this act of courage she became the first person to encounter the risen Christ. Jesus then sent this woman to bring the good news to the others.

Pause

As women in the church, may you show leadership in the face of doubt and dejection. Continue to believe in the promises of Christ so that you may be a wellspring of healing and hope in a broken world.

Mary the mother of Jesus (first voice): Mary as a young mother said yes to the will of God. She nurtured the divine in the human and in her womb bore God to the world. Mary followed her son all the way to the cross.

Pause

As women in the church, say 'yes' to God's word and nurture the divine presence in the human. As mothers, build a church that is home to all.

When these texts have been read each individual goes before the leader/elder who places the open bible over her head and says: 'God's word has been sown in your heart. You are God's word.'

Rite of Affirmation for Men

All men who are not ordained are called forward and stand in front of the assembly.

Jeremiah (second voice): As a young man Jeremiah was told by God 'before I formed you in the womb I knew you, before you came to birth I consecrated you'. Jeremiah was consecrated as a prophet and became a man who courageously spoke the truth. Many did not want to hear what he said because he condemned the wrongdoer and gave hope to the outcast.

Pause

As men, the world tells you to be powerful, to accumulate wealth and popularity. It tells you to be successful, to do well for yourself. May you be blessed like Jeremiah as prophet and speaker of the truth. Tell the world that the voice of the Spirit says be charitable, be merciful, forgive those who wrong you, and be honest and just in your dealings always.

Moses (first voice): When the Hebrews were slaves in Egypt they cried out to God to free them. God called Moses to liberate his people. He used no weapons, had no army, yet the spirit of the warrior within him fought and challenged the powers that held the people in bondage. God blessed the courage of this man and empowered him to lead the Hebrews through the waters of the Red Sea and into freedom.

Pause

As men, may God bless you with a brave heart to fight for the liberation of men and women from the oppression of injustice and despair.

John the Baptist (second voice): John the Baptist wore a garment of camel skin and he lived on locusts and wild honey. His home was the wilderness and his work was to preach repentance and to baptise in the waters of the Jordan. He was an outcast and lived alone, yet this man prepared the way for the Lord. It was this wild man that announced the coming of Christ into the world.

Pause

As men, may you find within yourselves the energy and courage to speak about Christ and prepare a way for his message in your homes, your places of work and in your communities.

When these texts have been read each individual goes before the leader/elder who places the open bible over his head and says: 'God's word has been sown in your heart. You are God's word.'

Rite of Affirmation for Priests

All men who are ordained priests are called forward and stand in front of the assembly.

Abraham (first voice): The name Abraham means Great Father. He was a man who had to leave his family, his father's house and his country to go to the land that God had shown him. He was to become the greatest of pilgrims. God blessed him and made of him a great nation.

Pause

As a priest, you too have sacrificed the comforts of home in order to lead your people as pilgrims on a spiritual journey. May God bless you and your work.

Solomon (second voice): Solomon was consecrated king of his people. God offered him any gift that he wanted. He asked for a heart to govern his people and to know right from wrong.

Pause

We pray that like Solomon, people will say of you:
You give justice to the poor,
You save children from poverty,
You free the lowly and helpless who call on you,
You take pity on the poor and weak,
And the souls of the powerless you save
For they are precious in your eyes.
(see Psalm 72:4, 12-14)

Paul (first voice): Paul who once zealously persecuted Christians was filled with the spirit of God to courageously preach Christ crucified. In the infancy of the church he formed communities of service and provided leadership to those who were lost and downhearted.

Pause

As priests, do all you can to preserve the unity of your communities. Bring reconciliation where there is division, comfort where there is loss, and hope where there is despair. And glory be to God whose power working in you can do infinitely more than you can ask or even imagine.

When these texts have been read each individual goes before the leader/elder who places the open bible over his head and says: 'God's word has been sown in your heart. You are God's word.'

8. Celebrating faith

There are no more important figures in Christian history than Peter and Paul. This ritual simply uses some of the scriptural words associated with them to help us reflect on our own faith. The first text is taken from Paul's writings.

There should be two readers reciting the texts alternatively with a short pause between each one. Ideally the two readers should stand at lecterns at opposite ends of the relevant space.

1 The word of God cuts more finely than a double-edged sword. It cuts between the marrow and the bone so that the truth can emerge.

2 What we preach is Christ crucified; a scandal for Jews and folly for Greeks, but for us, who believe, the wisdom and the glory of God. For God's foolishness is wiser than human wisdom, and God's weakness is stronger than human strength.

1 It is when I am weak that I am strong, for I feel the power of Christ shining through my human weakness.

2 I, Paul, appointed by God to be an apostle, send greetings to the church of God in Corinth, to the holy people of Jesus Christ who are called to take their place among all the saints everywhere. May God our Father and the Lord Jesus Christ send you grace and peace.

1 Nothing can ever come between us and the love of God made visible in Christ Jesus our Lord. No angel, no power, no division, no fear can ever separate us from the love of God.

2 The blessing cup that we bless is a communion with the blood of Christ and the bread that we break is a communion with the body of Christ. Because there is only one loaf means that we, though many, are one body because we all share the one loaf and the one cup.

1   Love is always patient and kind, it is never jealous. Love is
    never boastful or conceited, it is never rude or selfish. Love
    takes no pleasure in other people's sins but delights in the
    truth. It is always ready to excuse, to trust, to hope and to
    endure whatever comes.

2   Are you people in Galatia mad? Are you going to surrender
    the power of the Spirit and become slaves again? Surely
    you realise that Christ died for you and that you are now
    free?

1   We are only earthenware jars that hold this treasure, to
    make it clear that such an overwhelming power comes
    from God and not from us. We are in difficulties on all
    sides but never fear; we see no answer to our problems but
    never despair.

2   I thank my God each time I think of you and every time I
    pray for you, I pray with joy.

*After the reading, a sword (or a very large knife) is placed in a
position where it can clearly be seen. As this is happening a reader
says:*

It is through human weakness and frailty that God's word
is spoken; for God's foolishness is wiser than human wisdom and God's weakness is stronger than human strength.

This is followed by a song or some music.

The following text is then read:

Peter's faith (according to John's Gospel)
*Three readers are required. This text can simply be read reflec-
tively or acted out as a role play.*

Voice 1: In the evening of the first day of the week, Jesus
    showed himself to his disciples. He turned to Simon Peter
    and said: 'Simon, son of John, do you love me?'

Voice 2: Yes Lord, you know I love you.

Voice 3: While Simon Peter and another disciple were standing outside the door of the high priest's house, the woman keeping the door said to him – 'aren't you one of that man's disciples?'

Voice 2: I am not.

Voice 1: Jesus asked again: 'Simon, son of John, do you love me?'

Voice 2: Yes Lord, you know I love you.

Voice 3: One of the servants turned to Peter and said: 'You are one of his disciples surely; didn't I see you with him?'

Voice 2: I tell you I do not know the man.

Voice 1: A third time Jesus said: 'Simon, son of John, do you love me?'

Voice 2: Yes Lord, you know all things, you know I love you.

Voice 3: A woman standing by the fire turned to Peter and said: 'You are one of his disciples. Why, you are a Galilean! Your accent gives you away.'

Voice 2: I tell you I don't know what you are talking about. I swear I never saw the man.

Voice 1: You are Peter and upon this rock I will build my church. Feed my lambs. Feed my sheep.

After the reading, a rock is placed in a position where it can clearly be seen. Then a reader says:

It is on the foundations of human weakness and frailty that God builds the church; for God's foolishness is wiser than human wisdom and God's weakness is stronger than human strength.

This is followed by a song or some music.

The leader then says:

Peter and Paul prayed as Jesus taught them. Let us join with them in saying the words that Jesus gave us:

All recite the 'Our Father'.

The ritual closes with a blessing in these or similar words:

> You are the salt of the earth,
> you are the light of the world,
> together we are the body of Christ.
> As a baby you were baptised in Christ,
> at seven years you were invited to eat from the altar of God,
> and later the church confirmed the gift of God's Spirit given to you.
> Go now from this holy place,
> treasure in your heart the wonder of who you are
> and may the words you have heard here ever echo in your mind.
> You are the salt of the earth,
> you are the light of the world,
> together we are the body of Christ.

A Ritual to Celebrate
the Threshold of the New Millennium

The year 2000 marks a special moment in the Christian calendar and needs to be celebrated appropriately. Rituals were used in traditional societies when an entire group was moving from one place to another or from one status to another. The jubilee year is a threshold moment for the church because it is a time when the community must define itself as Christian before entering a new millennium full of uncertainties. Nations and organisations will prepare elaborate ceremonies celebrating the technological achievements of humankind. However, it is up to Christian communities to redress an overly secularised definition of the jubilee year. Christian communities must sing and dance and proclaim in word and symbol the true wonder of the jubilee, the coming of Christ into the world.

The ritual for the jubilee year outlined here can be adapted to any setting or environment as it is only proposed as a guide. It could take place in a particular community anytime between Advent 1999 and Christmas 2000. The obvious times are during Advent and Christmas 1999 or during Easter, Pentecost or Christmas 2000. If a parish or some other Christian community sets aside a special time of celebration during the jubilee year then it might end with this ritual.

The celebration revolves around the symbols of baptism. The intention is to help Christians face the opportunities and threats of the new millennium by revisiting the power of their own baptism.

Location

A large open space is required. A church is perfectly suitable provided that the pews can be moved to the side; if they are fixed to the floor this poses a problem. The whole ritual could be held outdoors. Even if it is held indoors it might be simpler to construct the threshold outside and to perform the last part of the ritual outside at the threshold.

Preparation

Perhaps one of the easiest things to do is to create an appropriate ritual setting. Night is preferred and the place should be lit with candles only. A candlelit space is rarely seen yet it effectively creates a different type of atmosphere. Seating also needs to be arranged and benches should be put to the side to allow for ease of movement in a large open space. Perhaps children from local schools could paint pictures of thresholds, doors and portals and these could decorate the walls. An actual threshold needs to be built and located in the created space in such a way that people can easily walk through it. Before the threshold is used people will be required to put water on their faces as they revisit that particular symbol of baptism, so containers need to be prepared. Another container is needed in which parts of the threshold can be burned.

Introduction

When the ritual begins it needs to be explained to people why at the threshold of the third millennium it is good to revisit the symbols of baptism. It should be noted that in baptism we receive our Christian identity and this needs to be reaffirmed so that we can move into another epoch with hope renewed. One of the symbols that can be dealt with here is light and darkness. The darkness can represent fear and an uncertainty of the future whereas Christ is the light and the light of the new dawn will overcome the darkness. The celebrations that will surround the millennium, as mentioned already, will differ greatly and a redress is needed to counter an overly materialistic interpretation.

1 Gathering

The celebration begins with music and song. As people gather there should be some background music, preferably live instrumental music.

2 Welcome

The leader welcomes those present and introduces the theme of baptism laying particular emphasis on the gift of the Holy Spirit. A suitable song is then sung.

3 Reflection

This is followed by the reading of the following text. Two readers are needed, one reads the spirit of the world and the other the spirit of God. In each case the spirit of the world comes first followed within a couple of seconds by the spirit of God; there is then a substantial pause (10-20 seconds) before moving on. Ideally the two readers should stand at lecterns at opposite ends of the open space.

1   The spirit of the world says that externals are all important – looks, property, possessions. You are what you have.
2   The spirit of God says that your looks and appearance can be very deceptive. You must look into the heart, into the depth of life to see who we really are.
1   The spirit of the world says that life is a test and success is everything. It abhors failure and disappointment.
2   The spirit of God says that failure can be more important than success. We can learn much even from the sad and more difficult times.

1 The spirit of the world says that the great problems – unemployment, ecology, violence – have nothing to do with me. I've just got to mind my own patch.

2 The spirit of God says that I am responsible for everyone, everywhere, at all times. There are no strangers in God's eyes.

1 The spirit of the world says that love is about things going well, in accord with my plans.

2 The spirit of God says that love is about giving of myself, even when I feel that I cannot.

1 The spirit of the world says that there is no such thing as forgiveness because there is no such thing as sin.

2 The spirit of God says that forgiveness is the greatest reality that we know. We sin, we fail, yet we can be freed to go on.

1 The spirit of the world says that honesty and commitment are impossible and don't really exist.

2 The spirit of God says that honesty and commitment are the only things that really matter in the end.

1 The spirit of the world says that the sick and the disabled are not really alive. Sickness and disability are disastrous.

2 The spirit of God says that the sick and the disabled are often those who are most alive for they know their dependence; they know that life is not in their control.

1 The spirit of the world says that death is the end of life and proves that life is futile.

2 The spirit of God says that death is not the end of life as the great spirit present in us is not extinguished but transformed.

4 Revisiting the Symbols of Baptism

Whoever is leading should briefly introduce water as a symbol. This should not be overdone, as symbols should be allowed to speak for themselves. Perhaps an appropriate story/poem could be read or scriptural passage, for example the parting of the Sea of Reeds in Exodus 14 or Jesus' own baptism in Mark 1. People should then be invited to come to the water and bless themselves. (If people are to immerse their heads there needs to be a source of flowing water). While doing so, they should say aloud, 'I believe in the Father, the Son and the Holy Spirit'.

Depending on the numbers present, this can take quite some time. Baptismal songs should be sung and instrumental music played during this time.

5 Scripture reading

When all have returned to their seats and the music has finished, two readers come to the lecterns to help us reflect on our own stories with biblical eyes. In each case a personal reflection comes first, followed after a pause by a biblical quotation; there is then a further pause before moving on. Ideally the two readers should stand at lecterns at opposite ends of the open space.

1 We are children of the earth, made of the same stuff as the stars; we are part of the beauty of the earth.
2 In the beginning God created the heavens and the earth. Now the earth was a formless void, there was darkness over the deep and God's Spirit hovered over the water. God saw what God had made and it was very good.
1 Think of the date you were born, the joy of your parents, family, neighbours and friends. Imagine yourself as a baby.
2 Before I formed you in the womb I knew you, before you came to birth I consecrated you.
1 Recall in your own mind the various places you've lived. Think of the houses, the places – go into each of them in your mind.
2 Wherever you go, I will go, wherever you live I will live.
1 Think of a couple of really happy moments in your life. Treasure them in your heart.
2 I want you to be happy, always happy in the Lord; I repeat, what I want is your happiness.

1 Allow moments of suffering and pain to enter your mind.
   They are part of who we are.
2 Come to me all you who labour and are overburdened and
   I will give you rest. For my yoke is easy and my burden is
   light.
1 Who are the people who accompany you? – family, spouse,
   children, neighbours, friends? Look at their faces now.
2 Did not our hearts burn within us as he talked to us on the
   road and explained the scriptures to us … and their eyes
   were opened and they recognised him in the breaking of
   the bread.
1 What do you hope for? What are your greatest expecta-
   tions, your cherished dream?
2 What we suffer in this life can never be compared to the
   glory which is yet to be revealed.
1 Where will it all end? What will happen in the future?
2 I saw a new heaven and a new earth … Then I heard a
   loud voice call from above: now I am making the whole of
   creation new.

*This part of the ritual ends with the singing of a song centred on
God's comforting of the people.*

6 Rites of Affirmation

Rituals should regenerate and give people new energy. The
rite of affirmation is intended to highlight the gifts of various
adults within the community: women, men, priests. Each
group (women, men, priests) is called forward separately.
They go to the front of the assembly where they stand facing
the leader/elders whilst the others remain seated. Then the
following texts are read aloud by the leader/elders.
Immediately afterwards they place an open bible over the
head of each individual and say 'God's word has been sown in
your heart. You are God's word.'

Rite of Affirmation for Women
All women present are called forward and stand at the front of the assembly.

Ruth (first voice): Ruth's mother-in-law was called Naomi and she had lost both her sons. In desperation and loneliness she decided to return to her homeland. She told Ruth that she had no more sons and that life with her had no future. However Ruth did not desert her mother-in-law. She said to her: 'Wherever you go I will go, wherever you live I will live.'

Pause

May you like Ruth be blessed with faithfulness and perseverance. As pilgrims on the journey of life, may you remain steadfast in your faith even in the midst of disillusionment and disappointment.

Mary of Magdala (second voice): After the resurrection, and whilst the followers of Jesus cowered in despair and fear, Mary of Magdala set out to tend the body of Jesus. Through this act of courage she became the first person to encounter the risen Christ. Jesus then sent this woman to bring the good news to the others.

Pause

As women in the church, may you show leadership in the face of doubt and dejection. Continue to believe in the promises of Christ so that you may be a wellspring of healing and hope in a broken world.

Mary the mother of Jesus (first voice): Mary as a young mother said yes to the will of God. She nurtured the divine in the human and in her womb bore God to the world. Mary followed her son all the way to the cross.

Pause

As women in the church, say 'yes' to God's word and nurture the divine presence in the human. As mothers, build a church that is home to all.

When these texts have been read each individual goes before the leader/elder who places the open bible over her head and says: 'God's word has been sown in your heart. You are God's word.'

Rite of Affirmation for Men
All men who are not ordained are called forward and stand in front of the assembly.
Jeremiah (second voice): As a young man Jeremiah was told by God 'before I formed you in the womb I knew you, before you came to birth I consecrated you'. Jeremiah was consecrated as a prophet and became a man who courageously spoke the truth. Many did not want to hear what he said because he condemned the wrongdoer and gave hope to the outcast.

Pause

As men, the world tells you to be powerful, to accumulate wealth and popularity. It tells you to be successful, to do well for yourself. May you be blessed like Jeremiah as prophet and speaker of the truth. Tell the world that the voice of the Spirit says be charitable, be merciful, forgive those who wrong you, and be honest and just in your dealings always.

Moses (first voice): When the Hebrews were slaves in Egypt they cried out to God to free them. God called Moses to liberate his people. He used no weapons, had no army, yet the spirit of the warrior within him fought and challenged the powers that held the people in bondage. God blessed the courage of this man and empowered him to lead the Hebrews through the waters of the Red Sea and into freedom.

Pause

As men, may God bless you with a brave heart to fight for the liberation of men and women from the oppression of injustice and despair.

John the Baptist (second voice): John the Baptist wore a garment of camel skin and he lived on locusts and wild honey. His home was the wilderness and his work was to preach repentance and to baptise in the waters of the Jordan. He was an outcast and lived alone, yet this man prepared the way for the Lord. It was this wild man that announced the coming of Christ into the world.

Pause

As men, may you find within yourselves the energy and courage to speak about Christ and prepare a way for his message in your homes, your places of work and in your communities.

When these texts have been read each individual goes before the leader/elder who places the open bible over his head and says: 'God's word has been sown in your heart. You are God's word.'

Rite of Affirmation for Priests

All men who are ordained priests are called forward and stand in front of the assembly.

Abraham (first voice): The name Abraham means Great Father. He was a man who had to leave his family, his father's house and his country to go to the land that God had shown him. He was to become the greatest of pilgrims. God blessed him and made of him a great nation.

Pause

As a priest, you too have sacrificed the comforts of home in order to lead your people as pilgrims on a spiritual journey. May God bless you and your work.

Solomon (second voice): Solomon was consecrated king of his people. God offered him any gift that he wanted. He asked for a heart to govern his people and to know right from wrong.

Pause

We pray that like Solomon, people will say of you:
You give justice to the poor,
You save children from poverty,
You free the lowly and helpless who call on you,
You take pity on the poor and weak,
And the souls of the powerless you save
For they are precious in your eyes.
(see Psalm 72:4, 12-14)

Paul (first voice): Paul who once zealously persecuted Christians
was filled with the spirit of God to courageously preach
Christ crucified. In the infancy of the church he formed
communities of service and provided leadership to those
who were lost and downhearted.

Pause

As priests, do all you can to preserve the unity of your
communities. Bring reconciliation where there is division,
comfort where there is loss, and hope where there is despair. And glory be to God whose power working in you can
do infinitely more than you can ask or even imagine.

*When these texts have been read each individual goes before the
leader/elder who places the open bible over his head and says:
'God's word has been sown in your heart. You are God's word.'*

This part of the ritual concludes with vibrant instrumental music.

7 The Threshold

A threshold marks the point at which a person leaves behind a
particular place and is just about to enter a new one. Used as a
symbol here, however, the threshold marks the point at which
the community leaves the certainty of the past along with its
shortcomings and failings to enter a Christian future of hope,
promise, affirmation and thanksgiving. Every community will
have its own individual stories that will make the threshold
meaningful for them. This could be a moment to recount the

way a community has been blessed in the past. So too, moments of tragedy need to be remembered. Depending on the community, the ritual at the threshold could become a focus for healing and reconciliation. Forgiveness is about healing the past and leaving it behind and the destruction of the threshold can be a potent symbol here. Walking through the threshold can simply be taken at the level of each person's own private memories, things unspoken of, yet in need of healing.

All present gather on one side of the threshold. The leader asks those who have prepared symbols representing the life of the community to attach them to the threshold. Each individual should say a brief word about the symbol before attaching it to the threshold. The symbols should suggest times of great joy and sadness, hope and despair for this particular community. Then the leader reads the following text:

Lord God help me to let go.
Life is an endless process of letting go;
In our birth we had to let go of the security of our mother's womb and emerge into a strange world;
In adolescence we let go of the innocence of childhood;
All of us have to let go of home, parents must let go of their children and children must let go of their parents;

Throughout life as we grow and mature we must continually let go of opinions, jobs, good health and ultimately of the idea that we are in control.
And, of course, in death we must let go of those we love.
Between womb and tomb life is an endless process of letting go.
Come, Holy Spirit, help me to let go so that even when the letting go is tearful and sad it will awaken me to the mystery and wonder of life.

Life is the greatest gift we have received and in the end we must let go of this gift.

We must let go of the past to let God be the God of the future.

Each person is invited to pass through the threshold individually. As this takes place entrance and recessional hymns can be sung, particularly those with a marching beat. Before passing through the threshold each individual reads aloud from a card held up in front of them:

I am not afraid of dying to the old; I am not afraid of giving birth to what is new.

The threshold should then be destroyed and burned so as to mark the breaking with the past.

8 Anointing

In a simple action, all present are anointed with chrism to remind them of their baptism and confirmation and to strengthen them as they face the future.

The participants approach the leaders who put oil on their foreheads and say: You were anointed in baptism like Christ as priest, prophet and king; God's favour rests on you.

9 Final Blessing

The leader blesses the assembly in these or similar words:

You are the salt of the earth,
you are the light of the world,
together we are the body of Christ.
As a baby you were baptised in Christ,
at seven years you were invited to eat from the altar of God,
and later the church confirmed the gift of God's Spirit given to you.
Go now from this holy place,
treasure in your heart the wonder of who you are
and may the words you have heard here ever echo in your mind.

You are the salt of the earth,
you are the light of the world,
together we are the body of Christ.

If the ceremony takes place at night and the fire in which the threshold is burning is outdoors, more fuel might be added to the fire and people might gather round it with some refreshments and music.

Texts for use in rituals

1. Letting go

This text should simply be read reflectively by one reader.

Lord God help me to let go.

Life is an endless process of letting go;

In our birth we had to let go of the security of our mother's womb and emerge into a strange world;

In adolescence we let go of the innocence of childhood;

All of us have to let go of home, parents must let go of their children and children must let go of their parents;

Throughout life as we grow and mature we must continually let go of opinions, jobs, good health and ultimately of the idea that we are in control.

And, of course, in death we must let go of those we love.

Between womb and tomb life is an endless process of letting go.

Come, Holy Spirit, help me to let go so that even when the letting go is tearful and sad it will awaken me to the mystery and wonder of life.

Life is the greatest gift we have received and we must in the end let go of this gift.

We must let go of the past to let God be the God of the future.

2. Fear

Each line begins with 'I am', 'you are' or 'we are'. This text is particularly suitable when read along with Ecclesiastes 3:1-8.

For adults:
You are not afraid of dying to the old,
You are not afraid of giving birth to what is new,
You are not afraid of planting,
You are not afraid of uprooting what has been planted,
You are not afraid of searching,
You are not afraid of keeping or throwing away,
You are not afraid of tears or mourning,
You are not afraid of laughter.

For adolescents:
You are not afraid of dying to childhood ways,
You are not afraid of giving birth to wisdom and courage,
You are not afraid of planting responsibility in your life,
You are not afraid of uprooting what needs to be changed,
You are not afraid of searching for the man/woman that is within you,
You are not afraid of becoming independent and free,
You are not afraid of mourning your break with the past,
You are not afraid of embracing the future.

3. I am

This text should simply be read reflectively by one reader.

I am the wind of the sea,
I am the wave of the ocean,
I am the wind that blows,
I am the fire that burns.

I am not afraid of dying,
I am not afraid of searching,
I have gone where I would rather not go,
I have drunk from the water of life.

4. The power of Paul's words

There should be two readers reciting the texts alternatively with a short pause between each one. Ideally the two readers should stand at lecterns at opposite ends of the relevant space.

1 The word of God cuts more finely than a double-edged sword. It cuts between the marrow and the bone so that the truth can emerge.

2 What we preach is Christ crucified; a scandal for Jews and folly for Greeks, but for us, who believe, the wisdom and the glory of God. For God's foolishness is wiser than human wisdom, and God's weakness is stronger than human strength.

1 It is when I am weak that I am strong, for I feel the power of Christ shining through my human weakness.

2 I, Paul, appointed by God to be an apostle, send greetings to the church of God in Corinth, to the holy people of Jesus Christ who are called to take their place among all the saints everywhere. May God our Father and the Lord Jesus Christ send you grace and peace.

1 Nothing can ever come between us and the love of God made visible in Christ Jesus our Lord. No angel, no power, no division, no fear can ever separate us from the love of God.

2 The blessing cup that we bless is a communion with the blood of Christ and the bread that we break is a communion with the body of Christ. Because there is only one loaf means that we, though many, are one body because we all share the one loaf and the one cup.

1 Love is always patient and kind, it is never jealous. Love is never boastful or conceited, it is never rude or selfish. Love takes no pleasure in other people's sins but delights in the truth. It is always ready to excuse, to trust, to hope and to endure whatever comes.

2 Are you people in Galatia mad? Are you going to surrender the power of the Spirit and become slaves again? Surely you realise that Christ died for you and that you are now free?

1 We are only earthenware jars that hold this treasure, to make it clear that such an overwhelming power comes from God and not from us. We are in difficulties on all sides but never fear; we see no answer to our problems but never despair.

2 I thank my God each time I think of you and every time I pray for you, I pray with joy.

5. The spirit of God and the spirit of the world

Two readers are needed, one reads the spirit of the world and the other the spirit of God. In each case the spirit of the world comes first followed within a couple of seconds by the spirit of God; there is then a substantial pause (10-15 seconds) before moving on. Ideally the two readers should stand at lecterns at opposite ends of the relevant space.

1 The spirit of the world says that externals are all important – looks, property, possessions. You are what you have.

2 The spirit of God says that your looks and appearance can be very deceptive. You must look into the heart, into the depth of life to see who we really are.

1 The spirit of the world says that life is a test and success is everything. It abhors failure and disappointment.

2 The spirit of God says that failure can be more important than success. We can learn much even from the sad and more difficult times.

1 The spirit of the world says that the great problems – unemployment, ecology, violence – have nothing to do with me. I've just got to mind my own patch.

2 The spirit of God says that I am responsible for everyone, everywhere, at all times. There are no strangers in God's eyes.

1 The spirit of the world says that love is about things going well, in accord with my plans.

2 The spirit of God says that love is about giving of myself, even when I feel that I cannot.

1 The spirit of the world says that there is no such thing as forgiveness because there is no such thing as sin.

2 The spirit of God says that forgiveness is the greatest reality that we know. We sin, we fail, yet we can be freed to go on.

1 The spirit of the world says that honesty and commitment are impossible and don't really exist.

2 The spirit of God says that honesty and commitment are the only things that really matter in the end.

1 The spirit of the world say that the sick and the disabled are not really alive. Sickness and disability are disastrous.

2 The spirit of God says that the sick and the disabled are often those who are most alive for they know their dependence; they know that life is not in their control.

1 The spirit of the world says that death is the end of life and proves that life is futile.

2 The spirit of God says that death is not the end of life as the great spirit present in us is not extinguished but transformed.

6. The community of Pentecost

This text can be read by one or more readers.

Remember the famous scene in the upper room when the disciples and Mary were waiting for the gift of the Spirit. Did you ever think much about the reality that they faced? In many ways that group, which included Mary the Mother of Jesus, was very akin to our gathering here today.

Some people in the upper room were doubtful about what it was all about; similarly some of us here are doubtful, wondering if we should be here at all.

Some were enthusiastic, bursting to tell the message to others; undoubtedly some of us are enthusiastic to get out there and tell people the good news.

Some of the disciples were very confused by everything that had happened to them; some of us are very confused by what has happened to us in our lives.

Some of the folk had grown cynical about the whole thing, believing that they had been fooled; maybe some of us have grown cynical too, having seen so much that disheartens us in the church and in religion in general.

Some of the disciples were broken by all the suffering and death they had witnessed; some of us are broken by life, by illness, by death.

Others of the disciples were worried and didn't know where to turn; some of us carry great worries about what the future holds.

Presumably some of the people in the upper room were bored, wondering if anything was ever going to happen; some of us probably find life tedious and wonder if it has any value.

And finally there were those who were deeply hopeful in the midst of it all, trusting in God's promise; equally there are people of deep hope and joy sitting in our midst today.

So if you count yourself somewhere, anywhere, amongst those who are doubtful, enthusiastic, confused, cynical, broken, worried, bored, hopeful or joyful, then take great heart for it was to such as these that the Spirit of God was first given. It was to a motley crew like ourselves that God gave the greatest gift: not to those who had all the answers, nor to those who had life all sewn up, but rather to those who were struggling with the realities of life.

Note: instead of saying 'some of us' or 'some people' in the second phrase, one could say – 'all of us at times are ...'.

7. My story with biblical eyes

In each case a personal reflection comes first followed after a pause by a biblical quotation; there is then a further pause before moving on. Ideally the two readers should stand at lecterns at opposite ends of the relevant space.

1 We are children of the earth, made of the same stuff as the stars; we are part of the beauty of the earth.

2 In the beginning God created the heavens and the earth. Now the earth was a formless void, there was darkness over the deep and God's Spirit hovered over the water. God saw what God had made and it was very good.

1 Think of the date you were born, the joy of your parents, family, neighbours and friends. Imagine yourself as a baby.

2 Before I formed you in the womb I knew you, before you came to birth I consecrated you.

1 Recall in your own mind the various places you've lived. Think of the houses, the places – go into each of them in your mind.

2 Wherever you go, I will go, wherever you live I will live.

1 Think of a couple of really happy moments in your life. Treasure them in your heart.

2 I want you to be happy, always happy in the Lord; I repeat, what I want is your happiness.

1 Allow moments of suffering and pain to enter your mind. They are part of who we are.

2 Come to me all you who labour and are overburdened and I will give you rest. For my yoke is easy and my burden is light.

1 Who are the people who accompany you? – family, spouse, children, neighbours, friends? Look at their faces now.

2 Did not our hearts burn within us as he talked to us on the road and explained the scriptures to us … and their eyes were opened and they recognised him in the breaking of the bread.

1 What do you hope for? What are your greatest expecta-
   tions, your cherished dream?
2 What we suffer in this life can never be compared to the
   glory which is yet to be revealed.
1 Where will it all end? What will happen in the future?
2 I saw a new heaven and a new earth ... Then I heard a
   loud voice call from above: now I am making the whole of
   creation new.

8. A blessing on leaving a Christian gathering

You are the salt of the earth,
you are the light of the world,
together we are the body of Christ.
As a baby you were baptised in Christ,
at seven years you were invited to eat from the altar of God,
and later the church confirmed the gift of God's Spirit given
to you.
Go now from this holy place,
treasure in your heart the wonder of who you are
and may the words you have heard here ever echo in your
mind.
You are the salt of the earth,
you are the light of the world,
together we are the body of Christ.

9. Take, bless, break and give

In the Eucharist bread is taken, blessed, broken and given.

In life we are taken, blessed, broken and given.

The priest takes the bread in his hands and blesses it during the eucharistic prayer;

then he breaks it and it is given to us as the body of Christ.

Through our birth and baptism we are taken into God's hands;

as the bread is taken, so too are we.

In life we are blessed by family, friends, love and joy;

as the bread is blessed, so too are we.

We are broken by failure, sin, pain and heartbreak;

as the bread is broken, so too are we.

In death we are given back to the mystery from which we came;

as the bread is given, so too are we.

When we take, bless, break and give bread to one another,

we believe the Lord to be especially present in our midst.

But we must learn to accept that in his memory

we will be taken, blessed, broken and given

for the life of the world.

10. Renewal of baptismal promises

Leader: Do you believe in God the creator of light and darkness, land and sea, heaven and earth, woman and man?

All: We do.

Leader: Do you cherish and protect the earth as God's creation?

All: We do.

Leader: Do you appreciate the gift of water which endlessly renews and sustains life?

All: We do.

Leader: Do you give thanks for the spring and the summer, the sowing and the harvest, the sun and the moon, the wind and the rain, the mountain top and the sea shore?

All: We do.

Leader: Do you believe that in the midst of a beautiful world we, like Adam and Eve, live in the shadow of temptation and evil?

All: We do.

Leader: Do you reject all that is evil?

All: We do.

Leader: Do you reject injustice, hatred, despair and bigotry?

All: We do.

Leader: Do you reject all that undermines and destroys the gift of life?

All: We do.

Leader: Do you believe that Jesus Christ is the Saviour of the world?

All: We do.

Leader: Do you believe that Jesus died for us on Calvary and was raised from the dead?

All: We do.

Leader: Do you believe that in baptism you became followers of Jesus?

All: We do.

Leader: Do you believe that when you were anointed with oil in baptism you received the gift of God's Spirit?

All: We do.

Leader: Do you believe that God's Spirit is present in humanity and that our destiny is to share fully in God's own life?

All: We do.

Leader: Do you accept the Christian identity that was given to you in your name at baptism?

All: We do.

Leader: Do you accept that your faith can only be lived with others in a Christian community?

All: We do.

Leader: Do you believe that the church, a community of saints and sinners, is the temple of God's presence in the world?

All: We do.

Leader: Do you take responsibility for the future well-being of the church?

All: We do.

Leader: Do you believe in the final triumph of Christ over sin, light over darkness, truth over lies, hope over despair, good over evil and life over death?

All: We do.

Leader: Do you today, in the presence of fellow believers, confirm the meaning and implications of your baptism?

All: We do.

Leader: Do you now promise to live your life in accordance with the Christian faith which we have professed together?

All: We do.

Leader: Then may God bless you and strengthen you as you bear witness to your faith.

11. Peter's faith (according to John's Gospel)

Three readers are required. This text can simply be read reflectively or acted out as a role play.

Voice 1: In the evening of the first day of the week, Jesus showed himself to his disciples. He turned to Simon Peter and said: 'Simon, son of John, do you love me?'

Voice 2: Yes Lord, you know I love you.

Voice 3: While Simon Peter and another disciple were standing outside the door of the high priest's house, the woman keeping the door said to him – 'aren't you one of that man's disciples?'

Voice 2: I am not.

Voice 1: Jesus asked again: 'Simon, son of John, do you love me?'

Voice 2: Yes Lord, you know I love you.

Voice 3: One of the servants turned to Peter and said: 'You are one of his disciples surely; didn't I see you with him?'

Voice 2: I tell you I do not know the man.

Voice 1: A third time Jesus said: 'Simon, son of John, do you love me?'

Voice 2: Yes Lord, you know all things, you know I love you.

Voice 3: A woman standing by the fire turned to Peter and said: 'You are one of his disciples. Why, you are a Galilean! Your accent gives you away.'

Voice 2: I tell you I don't know what you are talking about. I swear I never saw the man.

Voice 1: You are Peter and upon this rock I will build my church. Feed my lambs. Feed my sheep.

12. Affirming the Christian commitment of women

Two readers are required.

First voice: Ruth's mother-in-law was called Naomi and she had lost both her sons. In desperation and loneliness she decided to return to her homeland. She told Ruth that she had no more sons and that life with her had no future. However Ruth did not desert her mother-in-law. She said to her: 'Wherever you go I will go, wherever you live I will live.'

Pause

May you like Ruth be blessed with faithfulness and perseverance. As pilgrims on the journey of life, may you remain steadfast in your faith even in the midst of disillusionment and disappointment.

Second voice: After the resurrection, and whilst the followers of Jesus cowered in despair and fear, Mary of Magdala set out to tend the body of Jesus. Through this act of courage she became the first person to encounter the risen Christ. Jesus then sent this woman to bring the good news to the others.

Pause

As women in the church, may you show leadership in the face of doubt and dejection. Continue to believe in the promises of Christ so that you may be a wellspring of healing and hope in a broken world.

First voice: Mary as a young mother said 'yes' to the will of God. She nurtured the divine in the human and in her womb bore God to the world. Mary followed her son all the way to the cross.

Pause

As women in the church, say 'yes' to God's word and nurture the divine presence in the human. As mothers, build a church that is home to all.

13. Affirming the Christian commitment of men

Two readers are required.

First voice: As a young man Jeremiah was told by God 'before I formed you in the womb I knew you, before you came to birth I consecrated you'. Jeremiah was consecrated as a prophet and became a man who courageously spoke the truth. Many did not want to hear what he said because he condemned the wrongdoer and gave hope to the outcast.

Pause

Second voice: As men, the world tells you to be powerful, to accumulate wealth and popularity. It tells you to be successful, to do well for yourself. May you be blessed like Jeremiah as prophet and speaker of the truth. Tell the world that the voice of the Spirit says be charitable, be merciful, forgive those who wrong you, and be honest and just in your dealings always.

First voice: When the Hebrews were slaves in Egypt they cried out to God to free them. God called Moses to liberate his people. He used no weapons, had no army, yet the spirit of the warrior within him fought and challenged the powers that held the people in bondage. God blessed the courage of this man and empowered him to lead the Hebrews through the waters of the Red Sea and into freedom.

Pause

Second voice: As men, may God bless you with a brave heart to fight for the liberation of men and women from the oppression of injustice and despair.

First voice: John the Baptist wore a garment of camel skin and he lived on locusts and wild honey. His home was the wilderness and his work was to preach repentance and to baptise in the waters of the Jordan. He was an outcast and lived alone, yet this man prepared the way for the Lord. It was this wild man that announced the coming of Christ into the world.

Pause

As men, may you find within yourselves the energy and courage to speak about Christ and prepare a way for his message in your homes, your places of work and in your communities.

14. Affirming the Christian commitment of the ordained

Two readers are required.

First voice: The name Abraham means Great Father. He was a man who had to leave his family, his father's house and his country to go to the land that God had shown him. He was to become the greatest of pilgrims. God blessed him and made of him a great nation.

Pause

Second voice: As a priest, you too have sacrificed the comforts of home in order to lead your people as pilgrims on a spiritual journey. May God bless you and your work.

First voice: Solomon was consecrated king of his people. God offered him any gift that he wanted. He asked for a heart to govern his people and to know right from wrong.

Pause

Second voice: We pray that like Solomon, people will say of you:

You give justice to the poor,

You save children from poverty,

You free the lowly and helpless who call on you,

You take pity on the poor and weak,

And the souls of the powerless you save

For they are precious in your eyes. *(see Psalm 72:4, 12-14)*

First voice: Paul who once zealously persecuted Christians was filled with the spirit of God to courageously preach Christ crucified. In the infancy of the church he formed communities of service and provided leadership to those who were lost and downhearted.

Pause

Second voice: As priests, do all you can to preserve the unity of your communities. Bring reconciliation where there is division, comfort where there is loss, and hope where there is despair. And glory be to God whose power working in you can do infinitely more than you can ask or even imagine.